THE ART OF
BEING A SINNER

THE ART OF
BEING A SINNER

JOHN M. KRUMM

THE SEABURY PRESS · NEW YORK

ACKNOWLEDGMENTS

Grateful acknowledgment is made to the following publishers and authors for permission to use copyrighted material from the titles listed—either in original form, shortened form, or slightly adapted to the purposes of this book:

Atheneum Publishers—Edward Albee, *Who's Afraid of Virginia Woolf?*, reprinted by permission of the author.

Constable & Company, Ltd., and J. B. Lippincott Co.—H. A. Williams, *The True Wilderness.*

Coward-McCann, Inc.—Thornton Wilder, *The Angel That Troubled the Waters*, copyrighted 1928 by Coward-McCann, Inc.; copyright renewed 1956 by Thornton Wilder; reprinted by permission of Brandt & Brandt.

Doubleday & Company—Austin Farrer, *Love Almighty and Ills Unlimited*, copyrighted 1961.

Wm. B. Eerdmans Publishing Co.—Helmut Thielicke, "The God of Ends," in *Out of the Depths*, translated by G. W. Bromiley.

Victor Gollancz, Ltd.—Dorothy L. Sayers, *The Man Born to Be King*; reprinted by permission of A. Watkins, Inc., agents for the estate of the author.

Harcourt, Brace & World, Inc.—T. S. Eliot, *The Cocktail Party.*

Harper & Row, Publishers, Inc.—Stephen Bayne, *In the Eyes of the Lord*; and Robert Payne, *The Holy Fire.*

Alfred A. Knopf, Inc.—Albert Camus, *Resistance, Rebellion, and Death*, translated by Justin O'Brien.

The Macmillan Company—Harvey Cox, *The Secular City*, copyrighted 1965.

Oxford University Press—Christopher Fry, *The Dark Is Light Enough.*

Random House, Inc.—W. H. Auden, *The Collected Poetry of W. H. Auden*, copyrighted 1945; and Robert Penn Warren, *Brother to Dragons*, copyrighted 1953.

Charles Scribner's Sons—Paul Tillich, *The New Being.*

To the congregation of the Church of the Ascension—
in particular to the residents of the house on Perry Street
where much of this book was written.

Preface

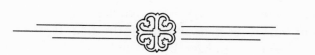

CHRISTIANITY is a religion with a commitment to historic experience, and the biblical as well as the theological analysis of the human problem generally centers in the idea of sin rather than in the idea of finitude. With this thought in mind, it has seemed appropriate that a book addressed to my Christian contemporaries should be one about sin. Since the book is written by a parish priest with no pretensions to serious or original theological scholarship, it obviously owes most of its ideas to others. Two great theological works of twenty-five to thirty years ago influenced my thinking in ways that cannot now be estimated, much less counteracted or changed. One was Reinhold Niebuhr's *Nature and Destiny of Man* and the other was Emil Brunner's *Man in Revolt*. I had been prepared for these two masterpieces by the persuasive teaching of Albert T. Mollegen at the Virginia Theological Seminary, and he will identify lines of thought in the book which owe more to his imaginative and fertile thinking than I can now recognize. Over the years these themes have also been illuminated by discussions with colleagues and friends. Two whose influence

7

has been most marked are the Bishop of Rochester, Dr. George W. Barrett, and the Reverend Dr. Howard A. Johnson. I have, no doubt, followed lines of thinking that they have suggested but in ways they would not altogether endorse. However, they know enough about forgiveness by this time to be generous and forbearing. It was reassuring, incidentally, to have Bishop and Mrs. Barrett read the manuscript and make helpful suggestions.

Most of all, the book owes insight to the people who, over the last twenty-eight years, have listened thoughtfully and carefully to my preaching and teaching and have done me the honor of discussing and even debating what I have said. The prevalent jokes about preaching suggest that no one listens to it. I have never been much amused by such humor, since I question its soundness in fact. It is an awesome experience and not an uncommon one for the preacher to realize how carefully people listen to him and with what seriousness they reflect upon what he says. To congregations in San Mateo, Los Angeles, Columbia University, and now at the Church of the Ascension, New York City, I am deeply grateful.

My secretary, Mrs. Ray F. Brown, has cheerfully and patiently typed the manuscript during a particularly warm and uncomfortable summer, and I salute her with heartfelt thanks. One of the privileges of being published by The Seabury Press is to work with Arthur R. Buckley, whose taste and tact and good sense are combined with a firmness which produces optimum results from his authors. This one is once again grateful and proud to have had his help.

JOHN M. KRUMM

The Eighth Sunday After Trinity, 1966

Contents

CHAPTER ONE

Sin in the Sixties

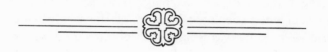

THE conversation at the reception was brisk, and the young clergyman was unprepared for the onslaught from the prominent newspaper publisher, a woman whose ancestors had been among the founding families of his parish. "I don't go to church any more myself," she said casually, as she introduced herself. "Every time I go, all they talk about is sin." Later he reflected that a good reply would have been, "I have the same objection to your newspapers." But that was an afterthought. At the moment he could only murmur a feebly jocular "tut, tut!" and pass on to more promising conversational territory. He did not forget the criticism, however, as Sunday after Sunday, in the twenty years that have passed, at every major service he has continued to urge the assembled worshipers "humbly to confess our sins unto Almighty God" or "to make your humble confession to Almighty God, devoutly kneeling." He is writing this book because he thinks the woman was

wrong and this is what he would have liked to have told
her.

In the year in which the comment was first made, the
doctrine of sin was having great currency in Christian
theological circles. It was in the midst of World War II,
and illustrations of human sin shouted from the pictures on
the front pages of the woman's newspaper. One of the
most acclaimed theological works of the English-speaking
world at the time was Reinhold Niebuhr's *The Nature and
Destiny of Man*, one whole volume of which dealt with
the biblical teaching about sin, a teaching which Dr. Niebuhr contrasted brilliantly with the more optimistic views
of the contemporary liberal philosophies. A whole generation—not only of theologians but of political scientists
and social philosophers and literary artists and many others
—took the Christian teaching about sin with utter seriousness for the first time in their lives. The publisher quoted
above was a minority voice; sin was in vogue.

THE CONTEMPORARY ACCENT

Has the vogue passed? Is sin no longer a major theological preoccupation? Some of the contemporary trends in
religious thought seem to imply that our mood of twenty
years ago was too somber and too gloomy, shaded under-
standably enough by the events of the thirties and forties
but scarcely appropriate for the more hopeful days of the
sixties. Harvey Cox, one of the more articulate and persuasive of the new-style theologians, claims that men no
longer ask "religious" questions but are preoccupied with
"pragmatic" ones instead.

. . . the questions with which we concern ourselves tend to be mostly functional and operational. We wonder how power can be controlled and used responsibly. We ask how a reasonable international order can be fashioned out of the technological community into which we have been hurried. We worry about how the wizardry of medical science can be applied to the full without creating a world population constantly hovering on the brink of famine. These are pragmatic questions, and we are pragmatic men whose interest in religion is at best peripheral.[1]

The contemporary accent undeniably is on human capacity and dignity and responsibility. "Man come of age" is the rallying cry of contemporary Christian thought. Modern technology has put into man's hands tools with the most awesome possibilities. Rather than shrink from handling them—dismayed by the sense of his own shortcomings, which the doctrine of sin represents—should not a modern Christian be urged to that kind of "boldness" of which St. Paul used to speak and set out to resolve the pragmatic questions toward which Professor Cox points him? If the Church is to talk all the time about sin, does she not thereby cast a kind of malaise over modern life from which the contemporary man is likely to recoil with the woman publisher's distaste?

There is considerable cogency in these arguments, and yet Christian theology can never speak just to the immediate mood or to the superficial aspects of its contemporary expression. Christian theology ought to reflect a wisdom derived from the crucial events of its sacred history, a wisdom tested and verified and corroborated by the long years of human experience. There may very well be periods— there seem to have been not infrequently in the past—when the Church's message has sounded archaic and irrelevant in the ears of the heedless and unthinking. The new theology in some of its expressions may indeed—in the current colloquialism—"swing," but the swing may be simply that of the pendulum. It is no indictment of the doctrine of sin that men do not like to think about it any more. The real question is: Does its teaching correspond to some of the perennial questions which, although suppressed in the urgencies of current pragmatic concerns, come to the surface to haunt and to disturb?

THE BIBLE'S LIVELY SENSE OF SIN

It is the contention of this book that the doctrine of sin is still the peculiar contribution of biblical religion to man's understanding of his life. It is a further contention that the Christians of the past who have advocated and exemplified the most vigorous and forthright handling of man's problems have been Christians who have also felt deeply the impact of biblical teaching about sin. St. Paul, that apostle of boldness who dared to challenge the Judaism of his fathers and the Roman civilization of his contemporaries with a new vision of life's possibilities and a new experience of its capacities, had wrested his confidence out of the depths of his struggle with the reality of sin. He found courage for every bold act in the face of the knowledge that he must die daily to sin. St. Augustine, the architect of the Christian social theories which inspired medieval civilization, summoned Christian men to a full involvement in the society of their times in the face of his conviction that the lust to dominate infected every human act. Disillusioned with the experiment in "Christian empire building" under Constantine, Augustine knew how pervasive and inescapable sin was, and yet he pointed men to their responsibility for the City of Earth with urgency and power. John Calvin, the breath-taking reformer of widespread areas of European society in the sixteenth century, began his miracle-working treatise on the *Institutes of the Christian Religion* with books on man's sin and the consequent limitations of his knowledge and wisdom as well as of his virtue and morality. A lively sense of sin seems to be no inhibition to vigorous, responsible social action.

Persuasive proof that a sense of sin need not inhibit a man from decisive and strategic political action of a revolutionary sort is found in the life and work of Abraham Lincoln. Though not apparently of a revolutionary temperament himself, he lived in a time of enormous and radical social change and was fully aware of the necessity and the inevitability of such change. Despite the fact that as President of the United States he was the center and focus of long-delayed and deeply desired transformations in the patterns of American life, Lincoln was never tempted to an exaggeration of the virtue or the wisdom of himself or his policies. The most notable mark of his words and of his political style was a deep awareness of the fallibility and frailty and sinfulness of men on both sides of the strident political and military struggle of which he was the center.

The more one reflects on the ways these Christians participated in the revolutionary movements of their times, the clearer it becomes that their style and posture was in large part determined by the liveliness of their sense of human fallibility and sin. The inevitability of the social revolution, for example, was traced to the deep-rooted self-centeredness of men and their institutions. The self-righteousness of the opponents was challenged and tempered by a reminder of their inescapable mutual myopia, and so the possibility of an ultimate binding up of wounds was kept open. The utopian hopes of what might be achieved by the revolution were treated with caution and restraint. It is instructive to recall that not a single revolution of human society has fulfilled all its hopes. It has been compromised and betrayed in many crucial ways. The revolution was necessary to clear away the debris of a collapsing social structure, but it did not usher in the promised utopia which had originally led men and women to invest their moral energy in it.

THE RESPONSIBILITY OF THE CHURCH

In our revolutionary time, some are urging the Church to become the "avant-garde" of the revolution. If this is meant to be a summons to the proclamation of God's judgments in our present history and to a preparation for the inevitability of radical changes in society, it is a legitimate summons and closely related to the sense of sin we have been discussing. But if it means that the Church is to instigate the revolution and give it strategic leadership, the summons is unrealistic, as a glance at ecclesiastical constituency and structure will make clear. Within the Church, of course, groups of men and women in special circumstances may perform this function, and one recalls with profound gratitude the leading role the Negro churches of the southern United States play in the movement for civil

rights and for greater freedom and opportunity for desperately depressed people. But one must be skeptical about the
likelihood that the Church as a whole can serve as the agent
of social revolution. A more modest—but perhaps no less
urgent—role is indicated. Perhaps it can maintain com-
munications across the barriers of strenuously opposed social and political programs and philosophies and avert the
intransigent self-righteousness which will bathe the revolution in blood and force it into paths of violence and destructiveness. And if violence and bloodshed come—as
Lincoln, at least, in his time was convinced that they were
to come as the punishment Providence inflicts upon a society which is impervious to calls to repentance—then once
again the knowledge of human sin means that the catastrophe has some moral meaning and that He who punishes
can be trusted also to rebuild and reconstruct. If our time
is a time of social upheaval—and who can doubt it—then
the teaching about sin has come into its own.

SIN AND THE NEW MORALITY

Another area of modern church life where a recognition
of human sin might be helpful is in discussions about "the
new morality." For all the merits of much that is being said
by the contemporary writers of this school, one is left with
the uneasy impression that it is being addressed to paragons
of perfect love and superhuman wisdom rather than to the
kind of ordinary sinners that Christians—at least liturgi-
cally—have always acknowledged themselves to be. One
of the more persuasive and articulate of the "new moral-
ists" has admitted that one might take exception to his posi-

tion on the ground "that it calls for more critical intelligence, more factual information, and more self-starting commitment to righteousness than most people can bring to bear. . . . [It] ignores human sin or egocentricity, and fails to appreciate the finitude of human reason." [2]

But having stated the misgivings of many of us, Joseph Fletcher only replies that a man can sin behind the façade of the law as easily as he can sin in the exercise of the kind of moral freedom which the author is endorsing. This misses the point of the difficulty. Of course, sin is to be found in the heart of the legalist as well as in the heart of the antinomian and equally in the heart of the "situationalist" (to borrow Fletcher's terminology). The question is whether the subtlety and pervasiveness of human sin which the Christian teaching has insisted upon ought not lead the prudent Christian to put himself under the tutelage of moral law and principle, not as a ceiling on his aspirations toward self-forgetful love but as a floor under his thoughtlessness, which will at least guarantee minimal decency and minimal orderliness in human society. Dr. Martin Luther King, Jr., has said that when he is asked why he continues to press for civil-rights legislation since he must realize that law can never create genuine love, his answer is, "No, law cannot make the white man love me; but it can keep him from lynching me, from barring me from the ballot box, from refusing my children quality education, and from denying me the status and dignity in the common life which is my birthright." Would the new moralist deplore such laws on the grounds that the justice which they create is something less than wholehearted agape-love?

We believe, further, that the doctrine of human sin is

a salutary safeguard when the flouting of law and principle becomes a moral necessity, as we would grant it sometimes does. The new morality seems to have gone a step beyond Luther, who advised men "to sin bravely," and advises them in our time "to sin cheerfully." Dr. Fletcher makes a significant amendment in a quotation, which he otherwise uses approvingly, from the late Alexander Miller. Professor Miller had interviewed members of the Resistance Movement in Holland and France who were committed and serious Christians and had discovered that they were forced to break most of the Ten Commandments in the line of their responsibility in the defeat of Hitler. Miller asked them whether everything then was permissible. "Yes, everything is permitted—and everything is forbidden." And Miller himself reflected, "If killing and lying are to be used it must be under the most urgent pressure of social necessity, and with a profound sense of guilt that no better way can presently be found." [3]

Fletcher, however, will not accept the word "guilt" and insists that "sorrow" is the proper word since, as he says, "such tragic situations are a cause for regret, but not for remorse." [4] But the doctrine of sin insists that remorse is always an appropriate human response to such a tangled situation. How does one know that he has acted prudently and lovingly and not—at least in part—irresponsibly and out of anxious self-concern? How can he help feeling remorse at the undermining of social order and human communication which wholesale lying and stealing and murder entail? And how can he be sure that he has not let the taste for thrill and an anarchistic dislike for authority lead him into unnecessary violence and destructiveness? The moral law against lying is a safeguard of the possibility of trust-worthiness and reliability in human relationships, and no one can break that law, even under the appalling conditions Dr. Miller described, without taking into account the possibility that he has not seen the situation accurately or has not responded to it wholly unselfishly.

The Christian teaching about sin, we have been saying, is a corrective to what might be called a kind of "romanticism" both in contemporary Christian social action and in present-day discussions of Christian morality. To recognize the reality of human sin is to take a somewhat more sober look at the nature of our world—in which modern theologians are quite rightly discerning God at work and summoning us to respond and share in that work—and to recognize the extent to which self-centeredness and rationalization may lurk within human behavior that likes to style itself mature and responsible.

THE DIMENSION OF CORPORATE GUILT

Now we must face criticism from another quarter. Is the Christian doctrine of sin not itself in danger of ministering to a certain kind of indiscriminate masochism and of substituting emotional self-reproach for a precise analysis of social ills and of prescriptions of such policies as may effect their cure? A few years ago on a college campus the chaplains of the several faiths drafted a statement for circulation among the faculty which invited them to sign their names to a manifesto on civil rights, especially for disadvantaged racial and ethnic groups in our American society. The statement spoke of "our national guilt" in the treatment of these groups, a guilt which the American academic institutions were alleged to share. These references to guilt provoked a sizable protest and resulted in many refusals to sign the manifesto. Several members of the History Department, for example, mindful of the disruptive effect of the idea of "war guilt" in European politics following World War I, declined to endorse the statement. A distinguished author of studies in the work of Sigmund Freud objected that the introduction of the idea of guilt was an unnecessarily disturbing one emotionally. A cool head rather than a penitent heart would be more useful, he insisted, in moving America toward a resolution of her racial problems. Another objection was that the idea of "national guilt" was too sweeping and indiscriminate. As one professor said, "It makes Governor Barnett and Eleanor Roosevelt equally guilty."

Several years ago Professor Charles Frankel wrote a book called *The Case for Modern Man*, one chapter of which was a criticism of Reinhold Niebuhr's writings about sin. One of Professor Frankel's difficulties was that the Christian idea of sin is too all-inclusive to be of any assistance in forming judgments about social and moral policies and actions. If we all have to confess our sins together, does it not imply an equality of status which flies in the face of our ordinary experience? In Jesus' parable of the Pharisee and the publican, the Pharisee really is a better man by all objective standards than the publican is, and why not recognize it? They should not have to say the General Confession together—or at least not with equal fervency.

These criticisms prompted the chaplains to take a more

careful look at the word "guilt." Their first reaction was
that it had ample Old Testament precedent. The denuncia-
tions of the prophets—at least, the earlier ones, before the
Exile—made no discriminations between relative degrees
of guilt and took for granted a social solidarity in which
all had in some sense sinned and all must share in the
punishment. Both Governor Barnett, of Mississippi, and
Eleanor Roosevelt have shared and prospered in an American economic and social structure which has been based on
racial injustice, traceable to almost the earliest times of
white settlement on this continent. In this sense they are
equally guilty. They differ, however, in their response to
this fact of guilt, and the difference might be expressed by
saying that one of them is ready to make a penitent acknowledgment of the national sin, whereas the other self-
righteously denies it. Unless this distinction is made, of
course, the idea of national guilt can lead to the sort of
indiscriminate condemnation of whole populations in international political reprisals for which the historians of modern Europe have an understandable fear and distaste. The
prophet Ezekiel felt obliged to rebuke a prophetic parable
from the past, "The fathers have eaten sour grapes, and the
children's teeth are set on edge." We should agree with
Ezekiel's criticism insofar as it is directed against a paralyz-
ing sense of past mistakes so deep-seated and prevalent that
all present corrective and redemptive activity is considered
useless. But Ezekiel, in his efforts to rouse a morally para-
lyzed people, went too far in the direction of what has been
called "atomizing" the moral life. Persons and institutions
in American society cannot isolate themselves from the sin
of racial injustice and claim that since their own record is

free from cases of overt injustice, they can claim the privilege of a clear conscience.

In T. S. Eliot's *The Cocktail Party*, when the news comes of the courageous and self-sacrificing martyrdom of Celia for the sake of native peoples among whom she was serving as a medical missionary, one of the characters says at once:

> But if this was right—if this was right for Celia—
> There must be something else that is terribly wrong.
> And the rest of us are somehow involved in the wrong.
> I should only speak for myself. I am sure that *I* am.

And another character echoes the same feeling by saying:

> Oh, Edward, I knew! I knew what you were thinking!
> Doesn't it help you, that I feel guilty too? [5]

The guilt of which these characters speak is obviously not the result of some specific act of immorality, the actual committing of what might be identified as a sin. It is much more a general failure to attain a higher level of virtue, to go a second mile or to turn another cheek. It is in this sense, perhaps, that we might speak of a national guilt. Not all the people of the nation have, of course, by their own deed perpetrated acts of racial injustice. The question is whether we do not all share in a general failure to rise to a new level of brotherhood, understanding, and mutual helpfulness. A flash of moral intuition which gives us a glimpse of the kind of nation we might have been may serve to generate the moral passion without which no thoroughgoing national reforms will ever be carried through successfully.

It is true, of course, that the disadvantaged people of America are probably chiefly interested in specific proposals for their welfare, in policies which will result in bringing them into the main stream of opportunity in the national life. Let us be quite clear that agonized contrition is no substitute for such proposals and such policies. But there are other needs in our society besides the correct policies—though they are indispensable, of course. There must be some way in which the solidarity and identity of the whole human community can be recognized and expressed. As we struggle to find the way to make the necessary changes in our social structure, there will be tensions and sharp conflicts of interest and of outlook. One of the ways to bridge those differences is to retain a lively sense of our human fallibility, our tendency to see issues from the perspective of our own privileges and advantages or lack of them, our persistent temptation to make absolute judgments and to dismiss those who differ from us as knaves or fools or both. Oliver Cromwell's famous entreaty that a colleague accept the possibility that he might be wrong—a possibility that Cromwell himself did not always keep before himself with sufficient vividness—is the kind of need a confession of sin will supply.

There is another need in our revolutionary society which the sense of sin may supply, and that is the emotional dynamics for sustained second-mile exertions. Abraham J. Heschel has pointed out that the distinctive contribution of the Hebrew prophets to the understanding of social ethics was an overarching sense of the divine pathos. The God of the prophets, Heschel argues, not only demanded justice but yearned for it as the fulfillment of the life of

his people. It was just this sense of "pathos" which the
prophets undertook to generate in the hearts of their
hearers. Amos was not a very helpful social analyst; one
shudders to think what specific proposals and policies he
would have had to put forward if he had been asked. If he
had been handed the state of Israel and given *carte blanche*
to run its domestic and foreign affairs, it is not likely he
would have been a conspicuous success. His contribution
was to create a certain "pathos" about the state of human
society, a lively sense of the ways in which men fail each
other again and again by a blunted sensitivity and a blinded
comprehension of each other's needs. Even when the right
policies are discovered, they can be administered with a
sense of detachment and condescension that will infuriate
those whom they are designed to help. This, in turn, will
prompt those wielding power in the society to ask in
frustration and injured pride in their magnanimity, "What
do they want, anyway? You give them help, and they ask
for more." When Jesus enjoined his followers, "Judge
not," he was obviously not suggesting that they did not
have to make decisions about policy or about the appropriate rewards and punishments by which any society must
administer justice. What he was warning against—as the
words about the mote and the beam in the eye make clear
—is a smug self-satisfaction which makes one's judgments
absolute. This is the "beam in thine own eye" which makes
it impossible to see clearly "the mote that is in thy brother's
eye." It is our blindness that makes even our attempts to
determine wise policy less than fully adequate for the needs
of our brethren. A deep apprehension of how greatly we
fail one another will prompt us to renewed effort and to

special acts of grace in propitiation for the massive social failure of the past. The penitent heart is no substitute for the cool head, but without it the cool head becomes too detached and manipulative and soon falters in its determination in the face of discouragement and ingratitude.

PENITENCE STILL A CHRISTIAN ART

These are some of the reasons why, despite the changed world of the sixties, sin still seems a relevant and illuminating way to look at life. In any case, it is written so deeply into the pages of the Bible and into the liturgical and devotional life of the Church that it would be difficult to excise it without major surgery which would disfigure the patient unrecognizably. Christianity is a historical religion, and it has always recognized a commitment to a historic experience, beginning in Judaism and continuing in the life of the Christian Church. It has been pointed out many times that the analysis of the human problem in the Hebrew prophets and in St. Paul as well as in most of the great theological giants of the Christian tradition—St. Augustine, Luther, Calvin, and contemporaries like Barth and Tillich and Niebuhr—is an analysis that centers in the idea of sin rather than in the idea of finitude or creatureliness. A world of finite creatures is judged by the God of Genesis to be "very good." It is corrupted by a sinful attempt by the creature man to "be as gods."

This understanding of the human situation is reflected in the worship of the Christian Church. Almost all Christian bodies include a confession of sin as part of the structure of their public worship. An exception may be made in the case of the Roman Catholic Church, where the confession of sin is individual and private but so important that it is a prerequisite for the full participation in the Mass represented by the receiving of Holy Communion. The chapters of this book are intended to rescue these statements of confession and repentance from meaninglessness and hypocrisy.

Beyond all this, a consideration of sin may hope to revive the observance of Lent. Despite the ingenuity of some modern churchmen who would want to emphasize what they style "a positive Lent," the meaning of the season as a time for penitence is inescapable. We have tried to face in this chapter the difficulties in the way of making penitence a possibility for a modern man. The chapters that follow represent an effort to do just that in a contemporary way of thinking. We have assumed that we must mean what we say in worship when we mention our sin and the need for penitence, prayer, and forgiveness at the hands of a loving and atoning God. Unless all this is understood by the man and woman of the sixties, a very important part of our worship is barren, if not hypocritical. This book is sent out to the Church in the hope that by learning aright "the art of being a sinner," we may restore to this act in our worship its former importance and luster.

Prayer of General Confession

Almighty and most merciful Father; We have erred, and strayed from thy ways like lost sheep. We have followed too much the devices and desires of our own hearts. We have offended against thy holy laws. We have left undone those things which we ought to have done; And we have done those things which we ought not to have done; And there is no health in us. But thou, O Lord, have mercy upon us, miserable offenders. Spare thou those, O God, who confess their faults. Restore thou those who are penitent; According to thy promises declared unto mankind In Christ Jesus our Lord. And grant, O most merciful Father, for his sake; That we may hereafter live a godly, righteous, and sober life, To the glory of thy holy Name. Amen.

CHAPTER TWO

The God to Whom We Confess

To CONFESS one's sins presupposes the reality of a God, and indeed of a rather special kind of God. If it is true that God is dead, then one of the least lamentable consequences is that none of us needs to worry any longer about confessing his sins. If there is no fundamental purpose or meaning in life to which it is obliged to conform, then there can be no violation of such a purpose or defiance of such a meaning. Sin in the biblical and Christian meaning of the term may be defined as the alienation of the self from the fundamental value and significance of life, from the mind and will to which all life owes its pattern and meaning. The Christian experience of penitence for sin is in itself a hint that God lives after all—despite the reports of his demise. When we feel—as men and women often do—that by our folly and willfulness and self-preoccupation we have failed not just ourselves or our neighbors but life itself, we are bearing witness to the pressure of God on our lives. Of course, sin as the Bible and Christian tradition understand it has as a part of its dreadful consequences an estrangement from the neighbor and a dissatisfaction with one's own existence, but does the experience not go deeper? Is there not a dim realization that even if the act or the attitude has only very little influence on the neighbor and even if we can soon persuade ourselves to forget our momentary lapse, we have nevertheless betrayed a meaning for our lives to which we ought to have been loyal? If this is a part of the sense of sin, as I think it is, then the "death of God" theology seems to have overstated its case.

So, if our sin is only against the neighbor or against ourselves, then there can be no such thing as secret sin. At least, the secret will be known to someone, for if no one knows he is being sinned against, then how could we say that sin was being committed? The psalmist says, "Lo, thou requirest truth in the inward parts." God may demand that of us, but our neighbor does not usually do so. Our neighbor is usually content if we keep our word, do our duty, bear our share of the common responsibilities with cheerfulness and good grace. Whatever inner resentments and grudging acquiescence we are guilty of will not —if it really is kept secret from him—bother him at all. (We are assuming that an inner reluctance to do the right thing never betrays itself by any slight hint, and that may be improbable.) If God is a God "unto whom all hearts are open, all desires known, and from whom no secrets are hid," then we can talk meaningfully about sin—secret sins unknown either to the neighbor or to the self but known to God.

GOD AND MAN'S FULFILLMENT

God must also be a God who cares about individuals if sin is to have any real significance. If God is content with general conformity to his purposes, if he is troubled only when and if the peace of the universe is disturbed, then as long as one's own personal life does not break out into open rebellion against the order of things, that person need not worry about his sin at all. Sin which is only inner agony and personal disquiet would not trouble this kind of a "justice of the peace" God. Only if he is deeply concerned with each man's fulfillment of himself in personal qualities such as love and faith, only then will the usual Christian rhetoric about sin be appropriate. God the policeman will punish infractions of the rules which keep the universe running harmoniously, but only the God of love, who cares for the personal and inner development of his children, will be concerned about the kinds of things we talk about when we talk in church about sin—failures in inward integrity, in steadfast faith, in abiding love. It would be just as foolish for me to go to a God who was interested only in the maintenance of a neat and orderly universe and confess my sins to him as it would be to go to the local precinct police captain and tell him about my secret resentments.

It is worth noticing that even a professedly secular modern man like Albert Camus experiences a demand from life for an inward integrity which is not satisfied simply by co-operative and constructive social behavior. Camus' great novel *The Fall* tells the story of a man whose behavior was impeccable but whose inner fears and anxieties and insecurities mocked his most altruistic endeavors. The lawyer, Clemence, who speaks throughout the novel, speculates on what it would be like if every man were required to put his true identity on his visiting cards. What a contrast there would be between professed role and real function! "Imagine the visiting cards: Dupont, jittery philosopher, or Christian land-owner, or adulterous humanist . . . I know mine—a double-face, a charming Janus, and above it the motto: Don't rely on it. On my cards, Jean-Baptiste Clemence, play-actor." [1]

Some critics have speculated that the reason for Camus' concern with such a high standard of inward purity is the Jansenist background of his ancestry. Jansenism, against the easygoing moral tone of eighteenth-century France, preached the deep and pervasive power of sin. Camus' experience is a secular way of saying that God is in some ways like a Father—one concerned because of love with our personal integrity and moral fulfillment. He is not only concerned with what we do but with what we are.

HIS MERCY AND TRUTH

On the other hand, there is no good confessing to a God who is implacable and unyielding in his determination to seek punishment. If the God at the heart of reality is a God who demands an eye for an eye and a tooth for a tooth, then all we can do is grit our teeth and take our punishment, though we may wish bitterly that we had some way to retaliate against this unfeeling tyrant. A readiness to talk about our sins in the mood of confession and contrition presupposes a certain kind of God—the God, as a matter of fact, of the Bible and the Christian tradition, a God who is described in the prayer of General Confession as "Almighty and most merciful God," a God of whom it could be said as by the psalmist, "Mercy and truth are met together."

Dr. D. R. Davies, in his book about confession of sin,[2] called attention to the striking way in which this prayer of confession addresses God: "Almighty and most merciful Father." When you think about it, that is a rather surprising combination of adjectives—"almighty" and "most merciful." When power is defined in the usual way—the power to impose one's will upon another—mercy, the sympathy which understands and extenuates, is not often its accompanying quality. Power breeds fear and resentment in the weaker party and tempts the stronger party to overweening assertiveness. When America was first undertaking her massive program of foreign aid some twenty years ago, Dorothy Thompson, in her newspaper column, warned America of some of the probable by-products of such a program. She pointed out that aid extended by a stronger power to a weaker one would almost surely be received with a certain amount of distrust and resentment rather than with undying gratitude and fervent good will. No weak nation will relish being reminded of its dependence on another, stronger nation; and no matter how delicately and tactfully the assistance is given, there will be just enough smugness and condescension and self-importance in the giving to produce envy and hurt pride. This wise warning might have been heeded and pondered by statesmen who have protested that the foreign-aid program has failed because it has not bought America the good will of the world. If foreign aid is understood to have as its single purpose the creation of healthy and stable national societies strong enough to resist tyranny and subversion, then we may well be content with the main results of it; and our understanding of sin will not prompt us to demand the impossible—that it generate in addition sentiments of deep affection and devotion. The fact that so many Americans display irritation over this aid shows how rarely power and sympathetic understanding go together and how curious is the combination in God of the two adjectives "almighty" and "most merciful."

HIS POWER NOT ARBITRARY

Yet power alone as the chief attribute of God makes sin an altogether justifiable—even if hopeless—rebellion against a celestial tyrant. This is the dramatic problem which John Milton faced in *Paradise Lost* and notoriously, for most readers, failed to resolve. The temptation in the Garden of Eden was precisely the suggestion that God was to be understood as naked and arbitrary power, asserting itself against man in order to deprive him of legitimate satisfactions, to restrict unduly his happiness, and to insult his dignity. The serpent assures Eve that God has no real care about human welfare; God's only purpose is to maintain his power and to resist man's sharing it with him or seizing it from him. He wants to keep man in slavish subjection;

that is why he forbids Adam and Eve the fruit of the tree in the midst of the garden. That is plausible enough to man, since man was created with the capacity for freedom and responsibility, and so the serpent's words fell on receptive ears. We can imagine how galling it was for them to walk past that tree every morning and have to look at the flaunting glory of that forbidden fruit, wondering what it tasted like, imagining the new sensations it held within its mysterious gift.

The short-story writer H. H. Munro, familiarly known by his pen name, "Saki," once attempted a story about the temptation of Eve, but it was so perverse he was never able to finish it and left it among his unpublished papers, where it was found by his sister after his death.[3] In the story, Eve —to God's incredulous surprise—refuses to heed the serpent's temptation. She is depicted as a complacent and acquiescent woman, well behaved, unimaginative, who believed in doing what she was told and was not about to risk losing the pleasures of the Garden of Eden for some nonsense about a fruit she could very well do without. To the serpent's dismay, not to mention the archangel's and God's, Eve cannot be budged. "Adam and I went into the matter rather thoroughly last night, and we came to the conclusion that we should be rather ill-advised to eat of the fruit of that tree." No one can reason with her. The archangel Gabriel tries to explain that the whole course of human history is being held up by her stubborn obedience, but he is tactless enough to add that a poem called "Paradise . . . er, well, Regained" cannot very well be written unless she yields; that, of course, only increases her suspicion. Finally God is reduced to sending all kinds of unpleasant blights and fruit diseases to render the rest of the Eden fruit highly unattractive.

"We shall have to eat it after all," said Adam, who had breakfasted sparsely on some mouldy tamarinds and the rind of yesterday's melon.

"We were told not to, and we're not going to," said Eve stubbornly. Her mind was made up on the point. . . .

Eve's mulish and unimaginative conformity does not strike us as a quality of the ideal human being. No wonder that most readers cheer on the serpent in John Milton's great poem. The very dignity of being human is at stake in a world where God is just arbitrary power. The story of human progress is the story of a certain kind of audacity in going beyond previously accepted limits of human endeavor and achievement. To draw a line around this tree of knowledge and put it arbitrarily out of bounds flies in the face of every human instinct for adventure and daring. Unless God is more than what we usually mean by absolute power, then the story of the Garden of Eden is just another version of the myth of Prometheus, and the rebel is the hero. Significantly enough, scholars tell us that in all likelihood the Aeschylean story of Prometheus had a sequel, now lost, in which Zeus modified his arbitrary ways. Certainly the God of the Bible is not just the arbitrary God of the Eden story.

Dr. Davies would redefine "power" in the case of God as meaning not so much the ability to crush the opposition of the other and to force one's will on him as the capacity to accept opposition, to turn its enmity to unexpected purposes and to achieve its transformation in the end. If God's power were of the usual crushing and overpowering sort, then the story of Eden would have been the last as well as the first chapter in human history. The transgressors would have been wiped out and the last vestiges of rebellion extinguished, and the loveliness of the garden would have returned to its pristine state with nothing to trouble its serenity. Modern men, beset by the tangled problems of a complicated, technical civilization, may well wonder why God did not follow that course and abandon the obviously unpromising project of a free-willed humanity. Why should an almighty God allow his weak and vulnerable and foolish creature, man, to flout his purposes and defy his meanings for life and get away with it? There are, of course, patterns and laws in nature that man cannot defy successfully. Someone says that no one breaks the law of gravity by jumping out a tenth-story window; he just illustrates it! But God does let men break other laws—laws of man's relationship to the basic patterns of spiritual life, his dependence upon God and neighbor. Such defiance does not disprove God's power, as the village atheist who, daring God to strike him head, walked away unscathed may have supposed. It does, however, redefine power.

We see some hints of this new kind of power in some of the intimate human relationships of life. There are homes, for example, in which authority is stridently and vociferously asserted. Children are commanded into an obedient conformity: "seen but not heard" is a favorite description. Things move more or less like clockwork, though there is a certain tension in the air, and the guest is likely not to feel comfortable despite the outward signs of enforced order. Usually at the authority center of such a home is an insecure and uncertain human being, obliged to reassure his nervous doubts about the status of the authority by an enormous fussiness over rules and regulations. One has, thankfully, visited in other homes where a certain amount of cheerful chaos was allowed to prevail and where the heavy hand of regulation and rule was not often felt— or at least not asserted—but where there was a genuine respect for parents and where no one really dreamed of challenging basic principles of thoughtfulness and mutual concern, and if such trespasses did occur, usually a quiet reminder served to set things straight. This may serve as a parable of what it means to be "almighty and most merciful." God's power is proved in the very fact that his world permits so much freedom. He allows so much liberty of thought and action that it is possible for some skeptics to doubt whether there is any authority at the heart of the world at all. Only a God who had great resources for winning over opposition and of creating finally the glad and willing obedience of the rebels could afford to be so permissive. A God who has such a deep commitment to our freedom is a God who will welcome the confession of sin as a step in growing maturity and responsibility.

HIS REVELATION IN JESUS

It is just such a God that the Christian has encountered in the person of Jesus of Nazareth. The picture of him in the Gospels—most strikingly in the earliest of the written Gospels, St. Mark—is of one who moves unassumingly and inconspicuously among his fellow men, never stridently demanding respect or obedience, never self-importantly advertising his own virtues or powers. Even his spectacular works of mercy—the restoration of sanity and wholeness of mind and body and total person—are muted and played down. "Tell no one." The excited recognition of the demoniacs that this is the Holy One of Israel is instantly rebuked. Sometimes he seems almost to be discouraging instant discipleship, putting up some barriers that will test determination and separate glib joining up from deep commitment. He tells stories which have a point only to those who have eyes to see and ears to hear. He seems never to have wooed or seduced or enticed a disciple in his whole ministry. There was no emotional excitement about it, no public relations, no staging of effects. He was not what the world would call a powerful personality. He left no mark on the contemporary history of the times. His mark was left only on the lives that opened themselves to him freely and willingly and gladly. The almighty power of this strange person was seen most of all in his willingness to put himself at man's disposal, to submit to whatever their fear and insecurity and pride prompted them to do to him. The climax is the Cross, where his power seems reduced to nothing, and he is taunted with his weakness by his enemies. "Come down from the Cross and we will believe you." But with a reticence dictated by mercy, he maintains his servant character with a power of courage and faith and forebearance and hope that has brought men to their knees for nearly two thousand years.

It was just this capacity to accept whatever life did to him without losing faith in its goodness and meaning that struck the men and women with whom he dealt and gave him his authority in their eyes. The strange thing is that

those who knew him best were prompted to see in his
weakness and his defenselessness the very power of God
himself. As his enemies closed in on him and the circumstances of life blocked every opportunity for achievement
and accomplishment, his mysterious power became more
and more evident. It was not that life couldn't touch him;
it touched him so deeply and so agonizingly that he cried
out in bewilderment and dismay. But in the depths of his
agony and loneliness he never turned against life or the
God behind life with recrimination or bitterness or cynicism or despair. He went on loving and caring and offering
himself until his last breath. It prompted Christian iconogra-
phy later on to depict him on the Cross in the robes of
royalty. His was a royal power to grant freedom and to
endure anything freedom might inflict in its willfulness and
rebelliousness and to win men's hearts finally on freedom's
terms.

In succeeding chapters we shall be asking more precisely
what sin is, but here we can see that sin is not the brilliant
defiance of crushing divine power by Promethean man. It
is the turning away of a man's heart from the love of God
which has no weapons but the power of love itself. It means
mocking the love of Christ on his Cross. It consists in
shutting out the power of the divine love from our hearts
and minds. And when we recognize sin in that guise, see
it for what it is as we do at the Cross of Calvary, then it is
not an occasion for celebrating our freedom but for la-
menting our hardness of heart. There is the danger of sentimentality in the rhetoric we employ. Our hymns ask us
"to mourn our sins," and reference is frequently made to
"acknowledging our wretchedness" and "weeping, fasting

and praying." A parishioner complained recently that she didn't feel that way at all about her sins, and I had to admit that she seemed to be bearing up under their burden with considerable cheerfulness. Such phrases will begin to mean something only if we can see the connection between our sins and the loving, suffering Christ. If he on his Cross is the clearest picture men can ever have of the heart and mind which is at the center of all reality, then our defiance of that love is the saddest fact about our human condition. We would not expect to "weep and fast and pray" because we had broken a rule or flouted some petty tyranny; but if we have broken the heart of God as men did two thousand years ago on the hill outside Jerusalem, then our prayer of confession is not too dramatic a way of expressing our dismay and our grief. The only way we can justly estimate the reality of the sin of man is to understand the depths of the love of God.

CHAPTER THREE

The Grandeur and Misery of Sin

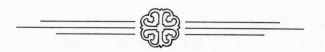

SIN is both a mark of man's high dignity and a proof of his weakness. Sin is a possibility only because man is given the responsibility of deciding for himself what it means to be a man. In the hit musical *Annie, Get Your Gun*, Ethel Merman has delighted a whole generation of theatergoers with a song called "Doin' What Comes Naturally." But that title—and the widespread popular thinking that lies behind it—misrepresents man's problem. It is not a question of whether or not to be "natural." The question is: What does "natural" mean in the case of a creature like man for whom a whole range of possibilities present themselves? To take the matter of human sexuality, which apparently the song in question is chiefly concerned with: What does it mean to be natural about sex? There have been all sorts of ways of expressing sexuality, and who is to say which of them is natural? The possibilities range all the way from the disciplined celibacy of a St. Francis of Assisi to the debauched promiscuity of a prostitute. Some forms of

Christianity have tried to argue that monogamous marriage
was the natural expression of sexuality, but this seems difficult to defend against the prevalence of polygamy and
polyandry in certain tribes, including the early Hebrews.
If one attempts to determine what is natural statistically—
that is, by a numerical average—then the definition changes
as statistics change, a fact which Dr. Alfred C. Kinsey
demonstrated to the dismay of those who would establish
natural morality by consensus. The point is that what is
natural can only be defined against the background of some
presupposition about the meaning and purpose of life, and
man quite obviously can thwart and pervert that meaning
and purpose in his assertion of his own freedom. Man alone
of all the creatures is given the task of discovering his
nature by himself, and that is his grandeur.

THE BIBLE ON THE FOLLY OF SIN

The similes used in the Bible, however, suggest that man
sins more out of weakness and folly than he does out of a
resolute determination to assert his freedom. The prayer of
General Confession, for example, says that men sin more
like silly sheep than like heroic Prometheus. There is not
much opportunity to observe sheep in our urban society,
but there is no report of their ever staging a brilliant defiance of the shepherd's authority. They just wander along,
heedless of danger, seeing one tuft of grass over there that
looks better than this tuft right here, never looking up to
see where they are going, and finally ending on some pre-
cipitous mountain ledge or in some menacing swamp where
they never in the world intended to be. Sin is weakness

more than it is sturdy defiance. The figure of Satan in the Christian mythology, on the other hand, represents sheer, brilliant defiance. He knows what he is doing, and he does it boldly and without a qualm. Men are not satanic, though they listen to Satan's suggestions. C. S. Lewis, in his brilliant book[1] of imaginative letters from a senior executive devil to a junior tempter on his first assignment, makes it clear that the Devil never really dares to show his hand. He is a liar, as St. John insisted, because he must seduce man's weakness rather than make a straightforward appeal to his rebelliousness. Man never takes his rebellion straight; it is always mixed with weakness.

It does not take great perceptiveness to see evidence in human affairs that men commit some of their worst sins by getting lost in the intricacies of life. Bertrand Russell once said that it was a hopeful sign for the future of the human race that, as he put it, "forethought more and more dominates impulse." One wishes that were truer than it is. In Robert Penn Warren's great poem, *Brother to Dragons*, there is a passage where the poet himself and Thomas Jefferson are imagined discussing a bloody crime which Jefferson's nephew committed in hacking one of his Negro slaves to death for a minor offense. Jefferson objects that the poet seems to be defending the outrageous deed, but Warren replies:

> I'd not defend him but I'd like to know
> Exactly how it was he came to the hour
> That is indefensible—for somehow we know
> That the last hour indefensible,
> When the stars sweat and the dear toad weeps in the hole,
> Is but the sum of all the defensible hours
> We have lived through.[2]

It has been pointed out that American commitment of troops to Vietnam began in 1961 when President John F. Kennedy, after the stormy confrontation with Khrushchev at the conference in Vienna, felt the need to demonstrate America's determination to resist Communist aggression vigorously, and so dispatched ten thousand troops to Vietnam. It is obvious that neither President Kennedy nor anyone else was able to employ Bertrand Russell's vaunted "forethought" to anticipate a situation in which four hundred thousand American troops would be taking the leading role in a war which would threaten the very fabric of South Vietnam society. We do not argue here the wisdom of the policy, but it is hardly the result of forethought; and if it is a mistake, it is clear that it is a mistake America stumbled into the way sheep get lost.

SINS OF THE FLESH

The Christian tradition talks about sins of the flesh. These are sins which Satan—if he really existed—would never feel any temptation to commit, since by the terms of the myth he is bodiless. But men and women have bodies and bodily needs which are obviously legitimate and must be attended to. So it is significant that Eve's attention is focused on the fruit of a tree, something obviously good to eat. The author of Genesis does not choose some purely formal act of defiance, as if God were to say, "Step over that chalk line and see what happens." Temptation takes the form of a fruit flourishing on a tree among all the other fruit trees of the garden. And the book of Genesis says, "When the woman saw that the tree was good for food. . . ." Who knows whether Eve, the thoughtful and prudent housewife, was not thinking that here was the perfect low-calorie, high-vitamin taste sensation to add variety to her breakfast tray? Men need food, and they need clothing and shelter and relaxation and some expression of their sexuality. So their sin is often an anxious attempt to provide for these needs with a preoccupation that thinks too much of self and not enough of others and our responsibilities toward them. We are led along unthinkingly, seeking one satisfaction of the body after another, transferring more things from the luxury list to the necessity list, all of it defensible except that it leads to an indefensible concentration upon self and self-satisfaction in a world crying out for sacrifice and renunciation as the prerequisite of meeting its needs. So some of man's sins are sins of the flesh, though the needs of his body are innocent enough in themselves.

HIDING IN THE FOREST OF THE PUBLIC

There is another thing I have been told about sheep, and that is that they go wrong oftentimes just by following other sheep. When Adam and Eve are faced by God with their disobedience, they can say, as if it were some justification of their offense: "Someone else put me up to it." "The woman tempted me and I did eat." "The serpent tempted me and I did eat." Because we need the support and fellowship of other people, we sometimes sin in the way the Christian tradition has described as "sins of the world." David Riesman has analyzed our society in his best-seller *The Lonely Crowd* as an other-directed society, caring most of all about an identification with the crowd around us. He reports an interview he heard on television in which a little girl was asked whether she wouldn't like to fly like Superman. She admitted that would be nice, but only if everyone else could fly too. "Otherwise," she explained, "you would be kind of conspicuous." In the same vein, a luxury automobile was advertised several years ago with the slogan, "For the man who wants to be inconspicuously important." More than a hundred years ago Søren Kierkegaard said that Adam hid in the trees of the garden but that contemporary man hides in the forest of that vague reality called "the public." It does not usually take much courage to sin. All one needs to do is to keep silent when a popular slur about some minority group is being retailed or some piece of obvious group selfishness is being justified. Follow the rest of the sheep, and you'll find sinning is no trouble at all.

OUR STUBBORN SELF-RIGHTEOUSNESS

If sin were only weakness, it would be unfortunate; but because man compounds the felony by his attempts at self-justification, it is calamitous. T. S. Eliot says in *The Cocktail Party* that man is engaged in "the endless struggle to think well of oneself." So a weakness that might easily be overcome stubbornly entrenches itself by posing as virtue. It is very difficult for man to renounce what Albert Camus called "the satisfaction of being right, the joy of self-esteem." So genuine, full-hearted repentance is one of the rarest things in the world. Even when the evidence of one's failures becomes almost unavoidable, resistance grows stronger.

A clergyman ministering in the southern part of the United States for the last fifteen years reports that southern churchmen do not expect their clergy to endorse segregation. Something deep down in the conscience knows that would be impossible for anyone professing to speak in the name of him who died "that all men might come within the reach of his saving embrace." But that deep-rooted instinctual realization does not accept the possibility that the clergyman may speak in favor of integration, for that would be too emphatic a demand for repentance. So the southern clergyman is expected, this observer believes, to avoid the subject altogether, and the formula that separates religion and politics, which no thoughtful, sensitive Christian ever really accepted absolutely, is invoked to make it all seem sensible and right. Man begins to stray like a lost sheep, but he soon sheds his sheeplike qualities as he refuses to admit his weakness and defends bitterly and ingeniously his "virtue" and his "wisdom."

Sin, since it is propelled by such a desperate determination not to admit its own reality, must infect every aspect of the human personality, even its highest and noblest faculties and capacities. Despite his rejection of the biblical categories, Sigmund Freud will provide the Christian analyst with all sorts of examples of sin's ingenuity and subtlety in masquerade and self-deception. W. H. Auden, in his poem "In Memory of Sigmund Freud," describes Freud's influence on modern man:

> Able to approach the Future as a friend
> Without a wardrobe of excuses, without
> A set mask of rectitude or an
> Embarrassing over-familiar gesture.[3]

One of the more obvious excuses—so obvious that one wonders that the ruse has been so successful—has been the use of certain kinds of smear words to defend social privilege. In affluent circles, no scorn is greater than that reserved for the "do-gooder." Yet what more innocent term could be imagined? Certainly the opposite would hardly be thought desirable—a "do-badder"! What is wrong with wanting to do good? Or consider the fate of the term "the welfare state." Its implications are intended to make all decent citizens shudder, and yet it would be hard to imagine a description of the state's functions more consistent with the Bible—or the United States Constitution, for that matter, which describes the function of the state in the unmistakable words "to promote the general welfare." The Gospel according to St. Matthew pictures the scene at the Last Judgment when all the nations of the world will be gathered together, and it is to be noticed that nations are being judged in this parable, not individuals. On what basis are they to be judged? The answer is explicit: have they fed the hungry, clothed the naked, ministered to the needs of prisoners, sheltered the homeless, and in other ways met the needs of the disadvantaged? It would be difficult to find a more comprehensive program for a welfare state than that.

There are, of course, spiritual and moral dangers inherent in the administration of assistance to people in need, both for the recipient and for the donor; but I should think it safe to say that most people who deplore "do-gooders" and "the welfare state" are resorting to the thinnest sort of disguise for the rather sordid fact that they do not want to part with their luxuries in order to meet the elementary needs of the underprivileged. John Kenneth Galbraith only stated the obvious—and yet how vigorously it is resented and resisted—when he said that affluent people quite naturally resist higher taxes because they have less need of the services and facilities which higher taxes provide: public parks and playgrounds, clean and safe subways, good public schools, adequate public hospitals, and all the rest.

We may have discovered here one of the justifications for the traditional Lenten discipline of fasting. It is very much out of favor, even in important ecclesiastical circles where it was once highly recommended. A sensitive conscience will, however, recognize the slippery ingenuity of the rationalizing mind and accept some discipline—simple and modest in scope perhaps—which may break the pattern (even for a little while and in little things) of caring too much for oneself.

Just after the war, Bruce Marshall wrote *Vespers in Vienna*, a story about British Occupation Forces billeted in a convent in the Austrian capital. One day an officer heard the news that the brother of the Mother Superior had been released from a Russian prison camp, and he tells her, quite sincerely, how glad he is to hear it. Later he reflects upon the depth of his concern about the young Austrian prisoner. How much would he have given for the young man's release? "A package of cigarettes? Well, of course; after all, a man's freedom is at stake. A whole month's cigarette ration? Well, hold on a moment, these are tense times, and one needs the relaxation of smoking. No cigarettes for a month would be pretty difficult. A month's liquor ration? Now look here, that's asking a lot for someone one has never seen. His month's army pay? Of course not. There is a family at home to think about." Then he sees what he is really thinking: that the extent of his charity and good will toward a fellow human being is measured by about one package of cigarettes and certainly not much more. Is it likely that such a feeble amount of the human quality on which the peace of the world depends is going to be sufficient to bridge misunderstandings and generate the good will to avoid more war and bloodshed? Perhaps it is just being realistic about our sin to establish a little pattern of self-denial which says "no" to the usual desire for comfort and well-being. The main result will probably be a deeper recognition of how selfishly we habitually think and act.

THE SUBTLETY OF THE WORKINGS OF SIN

Man's sin constitutes a stubborn problem because it is never just weakness, but weakness self-righteously defended and made into virtue. Two examples come to mind. One is the thesis of Herbert Butterfield, of Cambridge University, that the great threat to world peace is the self-righteousness of the two major powers, Russia and the United States (today he would add China to the list), which makes it impossible for them to negotiate through diplomatic channels for the resolution of the problems of world peace.[4] Diplomacy, Dr. Butterfield argues, is morally permissible only on the assumption that no nation by itself can quite do justice to the other nation's legitimate interests. Diplomacy is treachery and betrayal if you are convinced you are unqualifiedly on the side of justice and truth; but if you suspect that your own commitment to virtue is not altogether unmixed and that, therefore, the other side has a case which deserves to be heard and represented in a final solution, then diplomacy goes forward to its assigned tasks.

If we had a livelier sense of sin and a deeper understanding of the subtlety of its workings, we should admit straight off that which ought to be quite obvious: that the American people cannot be expected really to understand the antipathy of Asia to the white-dominated world of the West. The late John Foster Dulles, speaking in 1942 about Japan, said something that American foreign policy has not always remembered: "The white communities which ruled Shanghai, Hong Kong, Manila, and Singapore were racially snobbish to an extreme degree. Resentment against indignities remembered over a long time provides the driving force for armies who exact a revenge multiplied many times." Obvious as it is, this simple fact of international life is usually ignored while America proposes to commit four hundred thousand troops in an Asian struggle and wonders why she is so persistently misunderstood and her presence resented even by people who have no taste for Communism. As a rule, no simple solution to international problems exists, but a willingness to admit the limitations on our wisdom and virtue and foresight and tact would lower the temperature somewhat and create an atmosphere where negotiation and compromise could be regarded as legitimate and morally desirable.

Another illustration of the intricate connection between weakness and self-justification can be found in the wry observation of Professor Reinhold Niebuhr during World War II. He was a convinced and bold advocate of American involvement in the war against Hitler, and he felt quite honestly that no sacrifice was too great to demand for the elimination of the appalling Nazi tyranny over Europe. But he confessed that when his income tax came due, representing the first impact of the war budget, the amount assessed was a good deal more than he would have voluntarily assigned himself as his fair share of the financial load! One sometimes hears the justification for the opposition to high taxation that much of the government's program should properly be left to the voluntary contributions of private citizens and that enforced charity is cold and without any merit. A lively sense of sin will see that as an ingenious piece of self-justification, compounding the myopia of the ordinary citizen, who will never by himself be able to estimate adequately what he ought to give for the needs of others in our highly complicated society. A Lenten discipline—admittedly representing a very advanced form of spirituality—might be, for example, to give thanks for the payment of our taxes, by which we are led to do more for the welfare of our neighbors than we could ever voluntarily imagine or undertake.

Man as a sinner is perversely displaying the grandeur of his calling to be a child of God. He cannot just sin in his weakness and let it go at that. If he sins, he must pretend somehow that it is virtue. Hypocrisy is a sign that man is not totally depraved in his sin—a topic we shall look at more carefully in our next chapter. His weakness might be cured, or at least its destructive possibilities mitigated, if he would admit it and keep himself sensitive to the evidences of it. But the worst part of his sin is that it will not let him confess it. So his grandeur is in part the cause of his misery. He not only goes astray like a lost sheep, but he insulates himself more and more within the walls of his self-esteem and impeccable reputation. And when God cannot reach him or touch him, his condition is desperate indeed. This is the tragedy of his sin.

CHAPTER FOUR

How Sinful Are We?

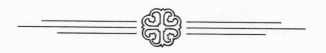

Most people feel, at least occasionally, that they have fallen
short of what they might have been, but the Church's language about sin seems to overstate the situation. The provost of the university where I was an undergraduate said
one time that, although he was not a member of any
church, when he went into an Episcopal church and heard
people saying, "We have left undone those things which
we ought to have done; and we have done those things
which we ought not to have done," he concluded that he
had found his crowd at last and was in the right company!
No one believes that he has lived up to his best all of the
time. But most men would not go so far as to say that they
were altogether bad—which is what the Bible and the
Christian tradition sometimes seem to be saying. My friend,
the university provost, would probably not want to endorse the phrase in the General Confession which says:
"And there is no health in us." The psalmist says: "Behold,
I was shapen in wickedness, and in sin hath my mother con-

55

ceived me." That's too strong, surely. I make mistakes; I fall short of my best; I have my little lapses—but I am not bad through and through. To put it briefly, most men would admit they commit sins once in a while, but they would not want to be classified permanently under the heading of "sinners."

THE MEANING OF "TOTAL DEPRAVITY"

We must not exaggerate, however, what the Christian tradition means when it talks about sin as our natural condition. It cannot mean that there is nothing good about us at all. If one means by "total depravity" that there is not a scrap of goodness in man at all, then it is a logical contradiction. If men really were totally depraved, they would be so bad they would not even be aware they were bad. The Hebrew prophet stood up and said that there was not one righteous man left in all of Israel. Of course, he forgot himself. The very fact that he was risking his reputation and popularity to challenge the morality of his nation and that a few people, at least, were listening to him was a sure sign that the nation still had important elements of spiritual strength within it. The most encouraging sign a man can have that he is not altogether lost and hopeless is his dismay over his sins. If he were all bad, he would never know it. The first step toward health is to admit one is ill, and the man who admits that knows something about health and wants to find it—and that is the clearest evidence in the world that his state is not hopeless.

Christianity means by total depravity that sin creeps in everywhere and infects every part of the personality and leaves its mark on every operation and function of the self. In southern California in the days of my youth, the onset of freezing weather ("unusual," of course) was combated in the orange groves by the firing of the orchard heaters, usually called smudge pots. Housewives in the neighborhood of the groves discovered that the oily smoke had a miraculous power to infiltrate even through the most tightly closed doors and windows and managed to leave its sooty, black film on curtains and rugs and furniture despite every precaution. Sin is like that. It gets into everything; it disfigures everything; it spoils everything. Total depravity does not mean that a man never does anything good; it means that, even when he does, his good is stained and spoiled and twisted and deformed. Bishop Stephen Bayne has described unforgettably how this can happen.

The minute our calculating, suspicious hands touch the things we do, they are turned into evil. . . . An act of unsought kindness to a man down in his luck can be a good and true and beautiful thing. But let us come home at night and contemplate it with satisfaction, and fondle it, and polish it, and put it on the mantelpiece for the family to admire, and suddenly it is no thing of grace and virtue at all but an ugly bit of presumptuous pride.[1]

Virtue may seek to erect impregnable barriers, but sin slips past, creeps around, sneaks under, and this is what is meant by total depravity.

THE ELUSIVENESS OF PERFECTION

Part of the reason why sin seems such a perennial problem is that our human ambitions are so lofty and so insatiable. Men insist upon reaching for the unattainable, dreaming of the impossible. In the musical play *Man of La Mancha,* Don Quixote sings a song about the vaunting ambitions and aspirations of man. They have been the source of all the great new movements of the human spirit by which frontiers and barriers have been breached. The penalty is that one must always feel the terrible drag of sloth and carelessness and insensitivity which bar his way to the sublime goal. Søren Kierkegaard once defined a poet this way:

> A poet is an unhappy creature whose heart is tortured by deepest suffering, but whose lips are so formed that when his sighs and cries stream out over them, their sound becomes like the sound of beautiful music. . . . And men flock about the poet saying: Sing for us soon again; that is to say, may new sufferings torture your soul, and may your lips continue to be formed as before.[2]

Part of the suffering of every artist is the realization that although men may find his work a thing of beauty, it falls below the level of perfection which he yearns to achieve. So their applause sounds ironic to his ears, for he is reaching out for an ideal and finding it eluding his grasp, partly through his own clumsiness, ineptitude, and insensitivity.

It is so also in the moral life. When the Bible measures the moral task as a task of love, it has condemned man's moral efforts to recurring disappointment and frustration. Love means identification and participation in and with the life of another, and yet, how formidable the barriers that separate us! A clerical friend of mine was calling on one of his parishioners not long ago, a charming and gracious woman of some wealth and social background, who fell to recounting the difficulties one has in these days with servants. "They have everything these days," she complained, "high wages, short working hours, days off, and yet they are more unsatisfactory than ever." My friend had the wisdom to say to her, "Yes, they seem to have everything they want, except, of course, the thing they want the most, which is not to be a servant." She saw the point at once and said, "Of course, I never thought of that. I wouldn't be a servant at someone else's beck and call for a thousand dollars a week." Here were people whom she lived beside day after day, yet an elementary truth about their feelings and attitudes had never occurred to her. Love calls for a sympathetic imagination that leaps across barriers to identify itself with the one who needs. But sin so often trips us up as we attempt the leap, and we never quite make it, and we end up condemning and misunderstanding and so raising the barriers even higher.

When Christianity talks about man created in God's image but now totally depraved, it is trying to account both for the reach toward the unattainable and the frustrations that keep it ever beyond our grasp. Original sin is so often misunderstood in so many ways that one hardly dares breathe a word of it in contemporary Christian thought. It is not, of course, the belief that because of a single act of disobedience in 4004 B.C. by a man called Adam and a woman called Eve, God decided to punish everyone ever since. Theologians speak about original sin in an effort to call attention to the fact that sin seems to be born with us and to be inherited from the world around us. Dean H. A.

Williams, of Trinity College, Cambridge, has given us two illustrations of how it works. He imagines one man who tells his story this way:

I was born of drunken parents in the worst sort of industrial slum. From my earliest days, I had to live by my wits. I always felt that it was only by being shrewd and calculating that I could hope to survive at all. . . . So it seemed to me that I was forced to stifle all sorts of natural instincts like trust and love and generosity. . . . So here I am now . . . nothing but shrewd and calculating, with an eye to the main chance.[3]

Dean Williams, by a second illustration, hastens to show that he is far from suggesting that original sin is found only among the socially and economically disadvantaged. He imagines another man saying:

My father is a member of Parliament. . . . I always had a good home and I was sent to the best school, and now I am a member of the best college in the best university. Naturally I admire my father's success. He has always been keen on success. . . . I felt I had to have it, so the self-assertive, success-grabbing me took charge of the rest. See me now at parties, cultivating the right friends, making the right remarks. Meet my fiancée, the right girl from the right background. Look at me in church now, asking God to help me go on being a success. I am not a whole man because my innate capacity for love and leisure and laughter and joy are all kept in chains by the little bit of me concerned with success and grabbing.[4]

In addition to Dean Williams' illustrations, which might be called the psychological version of original sin, there is the social version of original sin. Strictly speaking, the phrase "social sin" is a misnomer. There is no mechanism by which societies can sin. What happens is that in certain social contexts, men and women make decisions and choices which frustrate the purposes of love. Reinhold Niebuhr, in the title of one of his earliest books, *Moral Man and Immoral Society*, suggested that men who are highly moral in face-to-face relationships become immoral in their relationships in wider circles. Consider the courteous gentleman who invariably steps aside to let a woman go through a door ahead of him, but who, once behind the wheel of an automobile, will force the same woman, now also behind the wheel of a rival automobile, to slam on her brakes and swerve dangerously into another lane of traffic in order that he may beat her to a traffic signal! A more tragic example with far more serious consequences is the matter of slum housing in our large cities. Men and women and children live in filth and squalor which is a hazard not only to health but to dignity and decency, not because the landlord is in his personal life a monster of depravity but because he has lost his soul in the intricacies and anonymity of a complex urban society. The owner never bothers to question the profit he makes; the agent is afraid of a loss of his job if the profit level is allowed to slip; inspectors are afraid to "stick their necks out" and risk reprisals from higher up. So it goes, each man making the not too monstrously wicked decision that combines with similar decisions to produce an evil which blasts human lives, cripples human potentialities, and makes the city an increasingly desperate place in which to live.

THE SOCIAL ASPECT OF SIN

If a man feels the Bible and the Christian tradition have exaggerated the enormity of his sin, let him recall that the most poignant confessions of sin in the Bible are usually in the first-person plural. The prophet cried out against the sins of Israel and Judah. In the liturgical expressions of penitence, the Church has most frequently spoken of "our sins," and the prayer of General Confession says: "*We* have offended against thy holy laws. . . . There is no health in *us*." Although we have said that, strictly speaking, there is no such thing as social sin, some of our most deadly sins are committed within the context of societies; and if a man has not committed any face-to-face sins, he will be well advised to ponder what sins have been committed in his name and with his consent—or at least without his effective protest—by his neighborhood, his social club, his church, his city, his nation, his economic class, his racial group.

Nor is it easy to see just how love may be expressed by societies that have as part of their reason for being the maintenance of their power and responsibility. The United States government cannot be asked to renounce her power and appear before the nations defenseless in order to fulfil the meaning of love described in the Sermon on the Mount by the disturbing words: "Love your enemies. . . . If any man strike you on the right cheek, turn to him the other also." The setting of the illustrations in the Sermon on the Mount is an unnaturally simple one—just two people confronting one another and being challenged to love in that direct and uncomplicated situation.

But the very existence of societies calls attention to a whole network of relationships and responsibilities which make the application of the illustrations of the Sermon on the Mount very puzzling and difficult. I certainly hope my banker does not take with absolute simplicity the injunction, "Give to everyone that asketh of thee!" So Reinhold Niebuhr has called the Christian ethic "an impossible ethical ideal." He does not mean, as he makes clear again and again, that it is irrelevant. What is impossible about it is that it demands an understanding of consequences and a purity of intention which man is never capable of mustering. In his anxiety about his own importance or virtue, he misreads the signs of the times or never really hears the needs of his neighbor fully described. More than he ever knows, he acts out of self-regarding motives to call attention to himself and to bolster his shaky reputation and to reassure his uncertain ego. The fact that even the great heroes of the human race can be debunked by subsequent historical research is a sign of how deeply infected by sin we all are.

WHERE OUR TROUBLE LIES

This is what the Christian tradition has tried to face up to in its doctrine of original sin. The very fact that sin is not a problem we ever overcome, that Sunday after Sunday, year after year, sometimes more than once a day we repeat again and again in the Church's liturgy the acknowledgment of our sins: this means that the center of the trouble is right at the heart of the person himself. His sin is not just some things he does once in a while. *Whatever* he does can be seen to be in part a reflection of a sin that has colored his whole self—mind, body, heart, will, intention, everything. The title of this book, *The Art of Being a Sinner,* suggests that our problem is not how to stop sinning but what to do about the sins we inevitably commit. In *The Cocktail Party,* T. S. Eliot has one of the characters say, "Your business is not to clear your conscience but to learn how to bear the burdens on your conscience."

That is why the First Epistle of St. John says, "If we say that we have no sin, we deceive ourselves, and the truth is not in us. If we confess our sins, [God] is faithful and just to forgive us our sins. . . ." It is puzzling that in the same epistle he says in another passage that no one who is born of God commits sin (cf. 1 John 3:9). How can both verses be true? The answer is that St. John is writing to rebuke a school of thought which held that sin was an impossibility for a man who had certain kinds of spiritual illumination. Not at all, St. John says. Nothing man possesses or does can guarantee him freedom from sin. Sin is overcome from outside the self, and only as a man turns away from preoccupation with his own spiritual illumination and his supposedly superior moral virtue and opens his life to the forgiveness of God, is he beginning to overcome sin. The worst sins are the kinds of sins manifest in the teachers St. John is rebuking: the pride and exclusiveness which deny love and compassion. No one who is born of God is likely to fall into that kind of sin which grows out of belief in one's own innate spiritual superiority. To overcome sin lies only in the power of God himself.

In this sense, spiritual health is, I believe, strikingly different from physical health. As I understand it, what medicine is trying to do is to release the inherent powers of health within the sick person's body, so that, in effect, he cures himself. The doctor protests that he never cured anyone; he simply removed some obstacles or overcame some infirmity so that the latent and frustrated powers of healing which the body itself possesses could function effectively. That is not at all the way spiritual health is attained. A man is spiritually healthy only when he is invaded and taken over by some purpose greater than himself that focuses his loyalty and captures his energies and enables him to forget himself altogether. We have intimations of that kind of experience in human affection, in a devotion to beauty in form or sound or color (hence people speak of "art for art's sake"), in commitment to some cause of social reform or human betterment. There is no health in him, but health can overcome him from outside of himself.

One of the most famous sermons of the nineteenth century, by Thomas Chalmers, was called "The Expulsive Power of a New Affection." His point was that just as some of the dead leaves of a tree never fall to the ground all winter long but cling to the branches and are only discarded by the new life of the sap rising in the spring and replacing them with new leaves, so the dead instincts of man's soul can only be expelled and overcome when something new and powerful and alive takes possession of that soul. No man can ever deal effectively with his own sins. His seeming progress becomes an occasion for new sins of pride and self-congratulation.

It has been pointed out that men can even boast about

their humility! So the Bible can speak of our deep enslavement to sin. But the mood of the Bible is not a wallowing in our inadequacy. This is the kind of reaction to sin which St. Paul once called "worldly sorrow which worketh death." We see this kind of a sense of sin in some of our contemporary novels and plays. It brings cynicism and paralyzes the nerve of significant moral effort. The "godly sorrow" which St. Paul contrasts to the "worldly sorrow which worketh death" is a sorrow which, as the adjective implies, leads a man to turn more wholeheartedly than ever before to God, to the center and source of his life and the meaning and purpose of it, and to trust him for health and for salvation. So Lenten penitence leads a man toward the story of how God bore our sins and suffered their consequences and can promise to overcome them if we will let him. But if God is to work his saving work, there must be some opening of the human heart, some lowering of the barriers, and to that subject we turn in our next chapter.

CHAPTER FIVE

The Hopefulness of Being Sorry

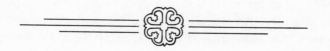

Many people today ask why healthy, capable, busy men and women should bother about sin. To them, concentrating on man's limitations seems like a defeatist and masochistic exercise. If men sin inevitably, then what good does it do to waste time regretting it? Why not concentrate on the hopeful, constructive, forward-looking aspects of human experience? In fact, these contemporaries would echo with approval the statement of the German philosopher J. G. Fichte, "I have no time for penitence."

THE REPRESSION OF GUILT NOT AN ANSWER

Even psychologists, however, who frequently are engaged in ridding troubled men and women of what are called "guilt complexes," testify that if guilt does exist, it cannot be swept under the rug. If someone is troubled by a sense of having failed and missed the mark, then he had much better face it rather than try to suppress it. And if he can believe that life has some resource within it for accepting human failures and mistakes and assuring one of forgiveness for them, then I suspect the psychiatrist would say, "By all means accept that assurance and get on with the business of constructive living."

I am not so sure that some contemporary psychologists would go as far as the Church goes in encouraging people to feel guilty. An American social psychologist speaks for many of his colleagues, I suspect, when he calls the sense of sin "a psychopathic aspect of adolescent mentality." But part of the problem here is semantics. Psychiatry would certainly have to admit that the sense of sin and guilt has at least led many people to seek psychiatric help. No one is likely to go to the trouble and expense of getting professional psychiatric assistance who has not been troubled first of all by some kind of remorse and regret over the poor showing he has made of his life hitherto. The first step which Alcoholics Anonymous requires is a confession that one is an alcoholic. In a similar way, the first step which leads to a psychiatrist's office and eventually, one hopes, toward psychic health is the confession that one has a psychiatric problem—and many clergymen and social workers will testify that that admission is oftentimes an exceedingly difficult one to elicit.

Biblical religion in a similar way is concerned that men and women face realistically the alienated and inhibited kind of life they are now living by reason of their sin. The problem of the men and women of the Bible is not that people have a "guilt complex" but that they have an "innocence complex"! Jeremiah, for example, is concerned that the people of his generation are so desperately trying to avoid facing the reality and the meaning of the sins of Judah. He pours out his anguish to God. "Then said I, Ah, Lord God! behold, the prophets say to them, Ye shall not see the sword, neither shall ye have famine, but I will give you assured peace in this place" (Jer. 14:13-14). Jeremiah is convinced, on the contrary, that this invitation to complacency is utterly unrealistic, and the burden of his message is intended to create a widespread guilt complex that will move the people to some such confession as this: "We acknowledge, O Lord, our wickedness and the iniquity of our fathers; for we have sinned against thee." The prophet is convinced that until this happens, nothing constructive and positive can begin to take place in the nation's life.

GUILT ABOUT THE WRONG THINGS

The problem is not that people are too guilt conscious these days. The problem may be that too many people are guilty about the wrong things. Dr. Harry Emerson Fosdick knew of a woman who heard read in church the Bible verse about having to give an account of every idle and foolish thing one had ever said. Apparently she had an overwhelming record for idle and foolish conversation, and she began to brood about it. All her conversation dried up (one cannot resist wondering whether this as a temporary handicap was altogether a disaster!), and she avoided seeing people and was by way of becoming a seriously withdrawn personality. Quite clearly, she needed to have some assistance—not, strictly speaking, to rid her altogether of a guilt complex but rather to get her to see her guilt in a larger context and meaning and to show her what forgiveness and living by God's.mercy really means.

Perhaps psychiatry helps people to eliminate the minor problems of guilt in order that they may be able to face and accept the fact that they live guilty lives inescapably on a major scale, and learn what to do about it. The Church owes psychiatry a debt that can scarcely be expressed for helping people to put their problems in a realistic perspective, for the Church does not exist for the sake of helping people face the troubles they think are their chief ones. One occasionally sees a column in the newspaper in which a person, often a clergyman, undertakes to give people advice about their problems. Such advice makes depressing reading. To hear the spiritual descendants of Amos and Jeremiah and St. Paul solemnly answering questions such as, "My mother-in-law has come to live with us; how can I get over resenting her?" is quite unnerving. In a world like ours, one wants to shout that both the letter writer and the mother-in-law might involve themselves in some real trouble in their community over the glaring problems of our society, and their mutual resentment might take its place far down the list of guilt priorities.

Psychiatry might also reflect on the fact that it owes to the biblical religion the fundamental faith that the center of the world's difficulties lies within the freedom of the human person and not in the structure of existence itself. The hopefulness of being sorry is partly the hopefulness that constructive and redemptive sorrow can tackle the fundamental flaw in human existence. In T. S. Eliot's *The Cocktail Party*, one of the characters says to the psychiatrist:

. . . I should really like to think there's something wrong with
  me—
Because if there isn't, then there's something wrong,
Or at least very different from what it seemed to be,
With the world itself—and that's much more frightening!
That would be terrible. So I'd rather believe
There is something wrong with me, that could be put right.[1]

If the modern world has thought Christian talk about sin
was morbid and defeatist, let him consider the alternatives.
A widely held one is that human existence is inherently and
constitutionally self-destructive. Several years ago I bought
a used car and, not being mechanically minded, I apparently did not make a good choice. The power steering
was always breaking down, the wheel alignment was in
perennial need of adjustment, and even the windows stuck
and couldn't be turned up or down. A friend of mine
passed eloquent, but accurate, judgment on the car when
he said flatly, "Let's face it: you got a lemon!" He went
on to say that nothing I could do to fix it would really be
satisfactory because the car was, somehow, basically all
wrong. Our guess finally was that a front-end collision had
put the whole frame of the car out of line. That is the
judgment of many people—including some of the world's
great religions—about human existence: "You've got a
lemon." The Buddhist, for example, is summoned to a way
of renunciation of all desire because the thirst for existence
is the source of suffering. The Buddhist saint is one who,
by losing his desire for existence altogether, is delivered
into the bliss of Nirvana.

Christianity will never allow us to assume that existence
is constitutionally bad. In the Book of Genesis, God is so

emphatic about the goodness of creation that he stops every
evening to pronounce it fundamentally good. The fault lies
not in our stars but in ourselves. There is something that
can happen to us that will be saving and redemptive and
able to make us whole. Consider the contrast between the
bitter advice of Job's wife, "Curse God and die," and Job's
own words toward the end of the story, "I repent in dust
and ashes." The first advice is hopeless; the response of Job
represents the hopefulness of being sorry. The first says
in effect, "You've got a lemon"; the second says, "I've mis-
handled life, but I recognize it and want to make a new
start altogether."

LUTHER'S PENETRATING INSIGHT

The hopefulness of being sorry is that it is the basic condition of health. This is what Martin Luther meant by
insisting on the centrality of the Pauline phrase "justification by faith." His meaning was not that instead of putting
forward works of morality and piety as a basis for justify-
ing his existence, man ought to substitute the intellectual
effort of belief or the emotional condition of feeling accepted. That has been a persistent misunderstanding of
Luther. A careful reading of his writings will make it clear
that for him faith is much more an acceptance of one's
own incapacity and inadequacy. It is what we might call
"the power of negative thinking." It is a whole 180-degree
rotation of perspective. It is an opening of one's heart and
life to God and to others. It does not mean hating oneself;
it just means forgetting oneself altogether in the glad service of life. Alexander Miller said that for Luther—who has

been described by one scholar as "a Copernicus in the sphere of religion"—"the question is not how I can attain my salvation, but how I can stop being concerned about it." [2]

Socrates many centuries ago came to a similar conclusion about wisdom. He was astonished to hear from the Delphic oracle that he was the wisest of men because he knew how scarcely he had touched even the outer borders of real understanding and wisdom. Then it was made clear to him that the truly wise man is the man who knows how little he knows and whose mind is open consequently to new truth. Luther's kind of faith is never, therefore, a possession, something one gets hold of and retains as a permanent virtue. It is always a death to an old wisdom or an old virtue and a readiness to receive new truth and new virtue. The most virtuous of men, the man really beginning to be free from the power of sin, is the man who recognizes in sorrow how far short of love's requirements he falls.

No story in the New Testament expresses this more winsomely and compellingly than the story of the prostitute who anointed our Lord's feet with her tears while he was dining in a Pharisee's house (Luke 7:36-50). The story, as Professor Paul Tillich has pointed out, makes no attempt to gloss over the woman's moral status. No one assures her that she just has a "guilt complex." According to the story, she is guilty—guilty of wasting life's possibilities and of cheapening the understanding of human sexuality in the community. Our Lord does not make excuses for her. He does not point out to the Pharisee that the fault lay largely with society or with her family and parental background, though that may well have been true. She is called "a sin-

ner," and the point of the story seems to be that her recognition of that fact led her to open her life to the forgiveness she had felt and seen in Jesus and led her to a deeper
understanding of God and of the meaning of human existence than the Pharisee ever dreamed of. Jesus contrasts
the cold and formal welcome the Pharisee gave him with
the extravagant emotion of the woman's welcome. "I en-
tered into thine house, thou gavest me no water for my
feet; but she hath washed my feet with tears, and wiped
them with the hairs of her head. Thou gavest me no kiss:
but this woman since the time I came in hath not ceased
to kiss my feet. My head with oil thou didst not anoint:
but this woman hath anointed my feet with ointment."

SORROW AND NEW DEPTH IN LIFE

Being sorry opens up wells of concern and compassion
and sympathy within the self and generates the grace and
magnanimity which are so necessary in a society where
men have sinned against each other for so long and can
live together only on the basis of mutual forgiveness. Dr.
Harry Emerson Fosdick once said of the prodigal son,
"out of the mine of his moral failure, he dug precious
metal." Dr. Fosdick speculated on the boy's new-found
tolerance and sympathy for other rebellious and impatient
young boys, his deeper understanding of the qualities of
forbearance and sacrifice, which alone sustain human relationships of love and affection, his more realistic estimate
of the importance of the excitement and thrills which he
had sought so single-mindedly that he forgot father and

home altogether. There is a sorrow for sin which can lead to new depth in life, new reality in human relationships, new hopefulness about the possibilities of meaning and significance even in the midst of tragedy and alienation and suffering. One way to look at the Church is to see it as the embodiment of this new principle of human community, as, in Dean Hughell Fosbroke's phrase, "the society of the forgiven." To understand the Church in this way is to anticipate and disarm some of the criticism that is often leveled against it.

One of the best-known literary heroes of our time is Holden Caulfield, the struggling and awkward but sensitive and perceptive adolescent hero of J. D. Salinger's novel *The Catcher in the Rye*. His observations about religion have the refreshing quality of naiveté which nevertheless penetrates to the heart of many theological questions. In a memorable passage he describes his reactions to the disciples of Jesus as they appear in the pages of the New Testament. What he says sums up the distaste many young people today feel for the Christian Church. The disciples are a pretty sorry lot, in his estimation. Again and again they misunderstand what he is trying to teach them; they fail him just when he needs them most. Young Caulfield is unmoved by the argument that we ought to respect the disciples because Jesus selected them. He had to pick up whomever he could on short notice, and such a random selection is, not surprisingly, pretty poor stuff. Caulfield admits he is impressed with the figure of Jesus himself but that only points up all the more sharply the glaring contrast with the small-minded and timid and craven disciples, whom Caulfield would dismiss as entirely useless.

THE SOCIETY OF THE FORGIVEN

This records an unmistakable impression one gains from the New Testament—an impression of a towering spirituality and sensitivity to life in the person of our Lord and of a correspondingly abysmal lack of appreciation and missing of the mark of these heights by his followers. It comes to its most vivid expression in the amazing choice of Peter to be the representative apostle. Of all the disciples who most often missed the point and let him down, Peter appeared to be *primus inter pares*. Yet it is this stumbling, impetuous, undependable, often abashed Peter who is given the charge "Feed my sheep" on that unforgettable morning on the lake shore. In Dorothy Sayers' radio plays, *The Man Born to Be King*, there is an exchange between James and John after the resurrection which faces this paradox of Peter's primacy and Peter's failure.

JOHN: Peter's more important. The church was to be founded on Peter.

JAMES: There again—No offence, Andrew, but that's always puzzled me. Why on Peter and not on you, John, who were his special friend?

JOHN: Perhaps because of that. I don't think you can found a church on personal friends and special cases. It's got to be less exclusive—more—what's that Greek word?—more catholic.[3]

With the memory of his abysmal failure on that calamitous night in the courtyard of the High Priest's palace torturing and assailing his conscience, Peter hears the Lord's astounding commission, "Feed my sheep."

But the apostolic commission is pre-eminently a commission to proclaim "forgiveness of sins," and who else can carry such a message with more poignancy or more penetrating persuasiveness than broken, remorseful, but forgiven Peter? In the Italian motion picture *The Gospel According to St. Matthew,* one of the memorable scenes shows Peter crouching against a wall, crying his heart out at the enormity of his betrayal of the one he loves more than anyone else in the world. Those tears are the warrant of his apostolic commission. Who will recount with more passion and comprehension the stories of the prodigal son and the lost sheep than forgiven Peter? Can we imagine some impeccable and morally immaculate Pharisee understanding why a man must oftentimes go the second mile or forgive seventy times seven? Not everyone can match St. John's understanding of what the coming of God into human life "in the flesh" really means, but everyone can understand what it means to be caught and compelled by the perfection of that Man for Others and then to fail him again and again and yet to receive just as consistently his pardon and his mercy and his commission to represent his love to the world. So Peter, not John, is the model of apostleship.

Dr. Fosbroke, in amplifying his definition of the Church which was cited above, writes: ". . . if we members of the Church would only rise obediently to the full realization of what it means to be members of the Society of the Forgiven, the Church would be enabled to minister so much more richly to the world at large the grace of reconciliation." [4] No tie binds men more closely together than the tie of a common sense of sin. In Christopher Fry's play

The Dark Is Light Enough, the Countess Rosmarin has taken pity on a rather disreputable, irresponsible, and undependable deserter from the army, taking him into her house and into the circle of her friends. As they settle down in her drawing room for after-dinner coffee, she senses the resentment, the suspicion, and the animosity.

> . . . Let us say
> That we are all confused, incomprehensible,
> Dangerous, contemptible, corrupt,
> And in that condition pass the evening
> Thankfully and well. In our plain defects
> We already know the brotherhood of man.[5]

When men know enough about their sin to be sorry for it, they are ready to accept one another on a deeper level than ever before. The Church represents that new depth in human community. There is no need to pretend here to an equality in virtue or wisdom that is chiefly romantic. The realistic equality is an equality in the need of forgiveness and in the gratitude and love which the assurance of such forgiveness can create. Here in the society of the forgiven is the most hopeful thing about our confession of sin. For here is a society that need not boast nervously of its prestige and power—boasting which causes only resentment and envy—but, resting on the mercy of the ever-loving God, can undertake "to minister . . . to the world at large the grace of reconciliation."

CHAPTER SIX

Who Shall Deliver Me?

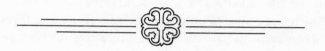

BEING sorry for one's sins is not, of course, by itself a healthy or a constructive thing. There is a kind of sorrow, we have already suggested, which may compound bitterness and increase isolation and alienation and become just as self-destructive as callous indifference or complacency. We see this kind of destructive sorrow in one of the chief figures in the Gospel accounts of our Lord's passion. He was a man who was as heartbroken as Peter but whose sorrow led to very different consequences. "He went out and hanged himself." The difference between Peter and Judas was not the fact that one had done better than the other in following and supporting and understanding his master. They both had failed him—Peter's failure was one of weakness, Judas' failure was the more determined and cold-blooded one of actual conspiracy—but both had to face the stark reality of their terrible inadequacy.

Both were sorry for what they had done. "Then Judas, which had betrayed him, when he saw that he was con-

demned, repented himself, and brought again the thirty
pieces of silver to the chief priests and elders, saying, I
have sinned in that I have betrayed the innocent blood."
It was a pathetic gesture, of course; and even if the authorities had taken back the money, it would not have undone
the betrayal or satisfied Judas' conscience. Nobody can
annul the consequences of his mistakes; they are part of the
stuff of history and go on doing their fearful work forever.
But when even his pathetic little gesture was refused, Judas
had only one thing left to do—the desperate deed of self-
destruction. So there was nothing hopeful about the kind
of sorrow that Judas experienced. It did nothing to open
his heart to the forgiveness and mercy of God. It only
turned him more in upon himself; and since he could do
nothing else, he did the one thing which self-centered men
might be expected to do—to exit from life by his own
deed, determined to the end to keep the resolution of the
issues of his life in his own hands. If he cannot justify his
own life by his own efforts, at least he can terminate it.
The other face of pride is despair.

THE CHOICE WE CONFRONT

The only real choice any of us has is whether to go the
way of Judas or the way of Peter. No one who faces the
record of the discharge of his responsibilities in life can
feel reassured about it. The deeper we go into an understanding of the demands life makes upon us the more we
discover that other people need a kind of integrity and
consistency and purity in our love and in our concern
which we just cannot create or sustain by ourselves. That

much is clear; what can be done about it? Peter let his remorse and grief lead him to a new level of faith and trust
in life and in the God who works graciously and redemptively within it. Judas let his remorse and grief lead to self-
destruction, just as many modern people seek escape in
alcohol or in mental breakdown or in a more decisive act
of suicide. What made the difference in their answers?

Despite the self-assured proclamation of the new "death
of God" theologians, we are bound to give an old-fash-
ioned answer to the question about Judas and Peter, and
it has to do with a trust in a gracious and loving and forgiving and powerful God. One of these contemporary
thinkers insists that "it is to the world and not God that
we repair for our needs and problems." [1] But where, in
the world he saw around him on that dreadful morning of
the first Good Friday, was Judas to look for a resolution
of the problem of his appalling sin? The world's reply to
his plea for help was summarized in the scornful dismissal
of the priests and elders, "What is that to us? See thou to
that." Even if he had been able to reach his condemned
friend and master, what consolation would it have been to
have heard of his human forgiveness? That would have
made the tragedy even worse—for how much more dreadful to have destroyed a loving and forgiving Jesus than to
have destroyed a hard and unrelenting Jesus!

St. Anselm in his treatise on *Cur Deus Homo* (*Why
God Became Man*) insisted that only God can deal with
the problem of human sin. At least one of the things he
meant was that man can live with the fact of his sin only if
he has an assurance that life as a whole has some victorious
way of absorbing his sin into its structure without violating

its moral character. The Gospels record Jesus' critics saying of his words of forgiveness, "Who can forgive sins but God only?" (Mark 2:7). They were quite right. The matter of sin cannot be resolved simply by the offended party mustering the grace to say to the offender, "You are forgiven." Sin has wider effects than the pain and grief caused to the individual directly assaulted. An example of heedlessness and callousness and thoughtlessness creates chaos in the texture of human relationships. It calls into question the whole enterprise of human love and makes it more difficult for men everywhere. The stain of self-assertiveness spreads throughout the entire fabric of human experience and darkens it. Forgiveness is never just a matter between two persons—the aggrieved one and the offending one. "Who can forgive sins but God only?" Only he who is ultimately responsible for the maintenance of life's meaning can undertake to pardon and extenuate violations of that meaning. So the sinner who needs forgiveness—and that will mean most of us most of the time—will persist in the question, "Who shall deliver me?" and not be put off by the sophisticated intellectualism that suggests his question has no meaning, since there is no longer one to whom such an inquiry can be addressed. He will understand that the very anguish of his sense of failure argues that somewhere there is a reality which maintains its pressure upon him. Only such a reality can deal with his problem. Only by steadfastly refusing to admit that this problem of sin exists can a "death of God" theologian maintain his curious position.

JESUS AND MAN'S SINFULNESS

Discussions about the divine nature of Jesus Christ ought to begin with this problem of how one can trust his words of forgiveness unless he speaks with an authority greater than that which belongs to an ordinary man. Some recent attempts to wrestle with the nature of Christ seem to emphasize his moral superiority.[2] No doubt this is part of the New Testament picture, but the Gospels make it clear —both at the beginning of his earthly life and at the end of it—that Jesus' uniqueness consists primarily in his power to cope with the problem of man's sin. The angel says to Joseph, "Thou shalt call his name Jesus, for he shall save his people from their sins." He himself says at the Last Supper with reference to the meaning of his approaching death, "This is my blood which is shed for many for the remission of sins." If his own sinlessness is an inescapable impression from the Gospel record, it can be said that this is a prerequisite for his role as the messenger and guarantor of divine forgiveness. Indeed, the power of the figure of Jesus in the Gospel is precisely that one so free from the anxiety and consequent self-assertiveness which is the root of sin should be able to sympathize so fully with those who are the victims of this universal human disorder.

This leads us to say something else about the figure of Jesus in the Gospels as the one who delivers man from the burden of sin, namely, that he must share the dilemma of the men and women whom he saves. This was, I am sure, the reason for the reiterated insistence of the Fathers of the Church upon the true and full humanity of Christ. Logic and reason lay with such heretics as Arius or Apollinarius, who wanted a simpler view than Christian orthodoxy came to insist upon. It was surely easier to affirm his divinity (or semidivinity, as Arius was careful to insist) than to make the kind of complex confession that Chalcedon finally made: that he can be spoken of as both God and man and that these two ways of speaking of him are not to be confused or equated.[3] The reason for the insistence upon his humanity was that only by such a God-man can the problem of sin be dealt with satisfactorily. When the church father Gregory of Nazianzus discussed the views of Apollinarius, who appeared to deny the full humanity of Jesus, his criticism was significantly that such a view meant that real humanity had not shared in the redemptive benefits of Christ's life and work. "For what he has not assumed he has not healed. . . . Let them not grudge us our entire salvation."[4]

Gregory was speaking here not as a speculative theologian but as a Christian who knew what it meant to be a forgiven sinner and who understood that such forgiveness implied a certain understanding of him who was the Saviour. He must be one who speaks out of a personal knowledge of what temptation means. An immaculate God who is of purer eyes than to behold iniquity cannot be expected to speak convincingly about forgiveness. He would be like the God recently described as confronting man in the Bible: ". . . the enemy God, present to man as terror or threat, comforting only in that he kept us from the worse terrors of life without him."[5] But surely this is a caricature of the God and Father of our Lord Jesus Christ. The precise point of much of the argument in the Epistle to the Hebrews is that Christians can "confidently approach the throne of grace, that we may receive mercy and find grace to help in time of need" because "we do not have a high priest who is unable to sympathize with our weaknesses, but one who in every respect has been tempted similarly to us" (Heb. 4:15). Hugh Montefiore, commenting on this verse, points out:

> The objection is here anticipated that one so exalted cannot properly sympathize with human frailties. . . . Jesus is not said to *sympathize* with these weaknesses in the sense that contemplation of them arouses in him feelings of pity and compassion. He sympathizes because he has, through common experience, a real kinship with those who suffer.[6]

Thornton Wilder understands the same truth and expresses it memorably in his play *The Angel That Troubled the Waters*. The scene of the play is laid at the pool of Siloam, where, at a certain hour of the day, the Gospel story tells us, an angel ruffles the surface of the water, and whoever at that moment is lowered into the pool is healed of his infirmity. In the throng of sufferers gathered expectantly around the pool one day, a physician is discovered. He suffers from an incurable disease, and, like the others, he is seeking a miraculous restoration of wholeness and health. But as he pushes forward, he hears the angel of healing speak to him:

> Draw back, physician, . . . Healing is not for you. . . . Without your wound where would your power be? It is your

very remorse that makes your low voice tremble into the
hearts of men. The very angels themselves cannot persuade the
wretched and blundering children on earth as can one human
being broken on the wheels of living. In Love's service only
the wounded soldiers can serve. Draw back. . . .

As he turns away from the pool, bewildered, he is caught
hold of by a distracted father.

May you be next, my brother. But come with me first, an
hour only, to my home. My son is lost in dark thoughts. I—I
do not understand him, and only you have ever lifted his
mood. Only an hour . . . my daughter since her child has
died sits in the shadow. She will not listen to us. . . .[7]

And so the physician learns the truth of what the Epistle
to the Hebrews says of the Great Physician, "In Love's
service, only the wounded soldiers can serve."

IN JESUS FORGIVENESS IS REALITY

The human Christ can persuade men as the archangel
Gabriel never could do that forgiveness is a reality. Part of
the reason is that redemptive forgiveness must never seem
to be a condoning of the sin, an acquiescence in its inevitability. This is a paradox, as we have already seen, that
although man must never imagine that he can say he has
no sin, he must also never cease to believe that by an
opening of life to God sin can have its root cut. But how
can he be convinced of that? The answer of the New
Testament Christian Church was the second Adam, the
man Christ Jesus, the one who met Adam's temptations
and responded to them by renewed acts of commitment

and faith. The power of sin is partly its ability to convince us of its inevitability. The Devil says to us in effect, "Why not yield now? You know you always do in the end." The only answer to that is to remember one who to every temptation replied with a new affirmation of his trust in God.

The first Adam in his temptation was prompted by doubt of God's goodness and power; the second Adam in his temptation meets every sly suggestion of the tempter with a reminder of God's centrality and priority and trust-worthiness. "Thou shalt not live by bread alone, but by every word that proceedeth out of the mouth of God." "Thou shalt not tempt the Lord thy God." "Thou shalt worship the Lord thy God and Him only shalt thou serve." Here is one who knows all about the reality of sin. Unlike the mythical figure of the first Adam, he is not an innocent. He meets sin on every side; he knows its consequences; he feels its terrible penalties by his remarkable identification of himself with others. Yet at every moment, in every crucial encounter, at every point where temptation presents itself, he does what the first Adam refused to do: he commits his life and his destiny once again into the hands of a God whom he trusts even in the depths of disappointment and disaster.

An analogy used frequently in recent theological discussion about the atoning work of Christ is that of military engagement. Bishop Gustav Aulén, reflecting partly the terrible European experience of military aggression and invasion in the first half of this century, has sought to revivify the ancient symbolism of Christ by his Cross putting to flight the demonic forces and breaking their power.[8] In the years after Aulén's book was published, a new aspect of military aggression became the daily experience of many Europeans: living under the power of an occupying army. Here is a further illustration and symbol of the power of sin—its pervasive and controlling influence, breaking morale and crushing hope. But to the occupied country there comes a flash of incredible good news—a liberating army has landed, has engaged the occupying forces in a crucial battle which fairly tested the strength of both sides, and has emerged clearly and splendidly victorious. The power of the occupying force is, of course, still very much a daily reality, but this crucial piece of good news has broken that power in the hearts and minds of the country's people.[9]

THE ASSURANCE OF ULTIMATE VICTORY

It is in just such an "in-between" time that Christians live with respect to the power of sin in their lives. St. Paul tried to describe it in several places in his epistles; but since it is such a paradoxical situation, he has not always been easily understood. Sometimes his meaning becomes clear just by the simple expedient of paying attention to the tense of the verbs. He says to the Romans, for example, "If we *be dead* with Christ, we believe that we *shall also live* with him" (Rom. 6:8). That speaks of a past event—a Christian's baptism into Christ's own self-renunciation; and of a future consummation—the ultimate sharing of Christ's resurrected glory.

But where, we may ask St. Paul, do we stand right now? The answer is that we stand within the assurance of an ultimate victory but not yet in the full possession of it. We have seen through the pretensions of the evil that besets us—the demoralizing frustration, the anxious and fearful efforts to secure our own defenses and to ensure our own reputation. We know how unreliable and self-defeating all such undertakings are. We are certain, too, about the ultimate possibility and power of an unquestioning faith in God's love and trustworthiness, because we have seen in Christ's resurrection how fully he glorifies a life which puts its reliance in him and in him alone. But there are many lesser engagements still to be fought as we try to capitalize on our Lord's great "breakthrough." And when the mopping-up operations grow fierce and wax hot, the Christian man remembers once again him who had no other power at his disposal but the power of his faith and no other assurance to cling to but the courage of his hope in God, but who with these weapons met the enemy in decisive encounter, disarmed him, and overthrew him utterly. "Who shall deliver me from this body of death? Thanks be to God through Jesus Christ our Lord."

Within the context of this faith in Jesus Christ—God and man, dying for our sins, raised for our justification— man's sorrow for sin does not deepen bitterness and increase alienation but leads out into a wider sense of identity with life and a surer confidence in its ultimate goodness. He finds a closer kinship with others who wrestle with sin's power. Dean H. A. Williams describes our mood:

"There, but for the grace of God, go I" sounds pious, but it speaks not of compassion but of superiority. Compassion says, "There, by the grace of God, I have been and I am." It is in this sense surely that we should understand St. Paul's words about Jesus: that God "made him to be sin for us, who knew no sin," or St. Matthew's words, echoing Isaiah: "Himself took our sins and bare our sicknesses. . . ." So when our lot is cast with somebody who is finding his cross, his desert, his poverty overwhelming, we are on holy ground. . . . Our identification with the other person brings to our lives and to theirs the power, the joy, the victory which is already ours and all mankind's in Christ Jesus Our Lord.[10]

CHAPTER SEVEN

Rescued by a Cross

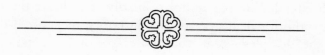

CHRISTIANS have always believed not only that it was Jesus Christ—God and man—who delivered them from the power of sin but that he accomplished this deliverance chiefly through his death and resurrection. When St. Paul is reminding the Christians in Corinth of the essentials of the message of salvation, which it has been his concern to bring to them, he puts the whole of his Gospel in simple and few words: "First and foremost, I handed on to you the facts which had been imparted to me: that Christ died for our sins, in accordance with the scriptures; that he was buried; that he was raised to life the third day, according to the scriptures." (1 Cor. 15:3, NEB)

The same simplicity of emphasis is reflected in the Gospel account which scholars tell us was the first to appear in its present form, the Gospel according to St. Mark. The details of the passage of time and of exact geographical movements which are passed over casually in earlier parts of the Gospel account are suddenly taken with

great seriousness as the solemn events of the Passion and
Death are recounted, beginning with the eleventh chapter.
It can be convincingly argued that St. Mark's interest in
Jesus' life and teaching before the climax in Jerusalem is
only in setting the stage for the denouement of the Cross
and the Resurrection. His healings and his parables are
both intended by the author primarily to indicate the hidden authority of his person, an authority recognized only
by the disciples—as in the confession of St. Peter—but
not to be shared by the crowd. (See Mark 1:44, and Mark
4:11-12, 34.) It has long been recognized how unsatisfying
the Gospel accounts are as providing a basis for a "life of
Jesus." Not his life, primarily, but the meaning of that
life to be seen chiefly in his death and resurrection: this is
Mark's focus of interest. We have a popular saying,
"Where there's life, there's hope," but, concerning Christ
and our sins, the New Testament—both Paul and the Gospels—would say instead, "Where there's death, there's
hope." Whatever significance Jesus Christ had for the
sins of men was centered primarily in his dying on the
Cross and his being raised from the dead.

THE MEANING OF JESUS' BAPTISM

While all this is true, his life and teachings also have
their place in the interest that the Gospels show in Christ
as the Saviour of the world. The events of Jesus' life and
the accents of his teaching are all marked with the sign
of the Cross by the Gospel writers. Some kinds of evangeli-
cal preaching have so emphasized the Cross—in itself a
sound instinct, representative of the New Testament itself

—as to neglect the life and the words which both made the Cross inevitable and gave it its full significance. A preacher once said that the life of Jesus Christ was "a crucial life" —a life with the marks of the Cross upon it from the outset. The same Christ who, St. Paul says, "died for our sins" also lived with the burden of them as his great preoccupation and spoke and taught with them as his recurring theme. Before we look more carefully at the Cross itself as the chief way by which the Lord dealt with human sin, let us look at his life as a preparation for the Cross and as dealing in its own way with sin's reality and power.

For St. Mark—and for the samples of early Christian preaching found in the Book of Acts—the first fact of Jesus' life which appears significant is his baptism by John the Baptist in the river of Jordan. His road to the Cross began when he joined other pilgrims to travel across the Judean hills to the Jordan valley to identify himself with the compelling preacher who was denouncing Israel's apostasy and demanding the dramatic act of baptism as a symbol of repentance and a recognition of the imminence of divine judgment. So Jesus joined his ministry onto the ministry of John, and the two were linked together in the memory of the Christian Church forever.

The significance of this initial step was something of a problem to some of the later Gospel writers. St. Matthew makes John demur, protesting that it would be more suitable if Jesus were to baptize *him*. St. John omits any reference to the baptism itself: the encounter between Jesus and John the Baptist is a recognition of the former's Messianic character. "Behold, the Lamb of God, who takes away the sins of the world." Why should Jesus the Messiah, the sinless one, the one who, more than anyone else the Evangelists had ever known, was free from the self-importance and self-concern that so marred the lives of others—why should this man undergo the rites of repentance? St. Matthew's answer is that so he desired "to fulfill all righteousness."

Nothing could be more illuminating of Jesus' understanding of sin or of how he believed it must be dealt with than his decision to be baptized. Sin is not to be dealt with as a matter of personal moral or spiritual hygiene in which one keeps himself scrupulously clean and uncontaminated from the infections in the world around him. Like John the Baptist, Jesus conceived of sin as a pervasive reality, a poisoning of the whole atmosphere of a society which enters into the acts of all its members to defile and to corrupt.[1] Sin cannot be dealt with by trying to immunize oneself against these influences, but by an entering into all the relationships where this defilement is at work and living in them penitently and redemptively. St. Paul wrote later that the Christ who knew no sin was made sin for us that he might cleanse and deliver us from sin. The burden he bore on the Cross he accepted first in the baptism in Jordan. He said in effect when he joined the pilgrims thronging to hear John and to receive his washing of penitence: "I belong to the whole human community, to its failures, its blindness, its insensitivity, its sin. I claim no immunity and no innocence. Wherever mankind sins and suffers I will stand and bear the penalty and endure the consequences." This is the baptism of which he spoke later to his disciples—"the baptism I am baptized with"—and which he promised and warned they must all share too. So his "crucial life" began to take its cruciform shape.

We find the same implications in his ministry to the sick, which occupied so much of his life's energies. He saw deeply into the meaning of sickness and saw it as a sign of sin's power, which it was his mission to exorcize. His healings were often associated by his own words with a rescue from sin. "Go, thy sins are forgiven thee." Such healings are spoken of as signs of the coming of the Kingdom of God and his righteousness. "If I by the finger of God cast out devils no doubt the Kingdom of God is come upon you." Quite obviously, in some cases, physical ills and spiritual disorder or sin are intimately connected. Sigmund Freud has helped us to see how anxiety and guilt take their toll in physical malfunctioning. By bestowing a power to live with guilt without succumbing to its destructive power, Jesus gave men a secret of health which in many ways anticipated the therapy of contemporary psychiatry.

THE INNOCENT VICTIM

But all this could be done persuasively only by one who himself bore the penalties and scars of sin in his own life and yet never allowed them to drive him to panic or to despair. "He saved others, himself he cannot save," jeered some of his enemies at the Cross. But this is true of any great physician. He must share in imagination and, consequently, in vividness and reality the disorders he seeks to treat. We have already seen how this theme has been treated in the New Testament and in contemporary literature. The only point from which anyone can help and save another man is *beside* him—not above or beyond him. The Great Physician must also be the Great Victim. The sins which are the special temptation of those who suffer

—despair, self-pity, self-disgust—are met and overcome by the one who suffers too, but who uses suffering to identify with others and with God himself. The great altar piece of Eisenheim depicts a repulsive and ugly figure of Christ on the Cross. His body is covered with sores, his joints twisted and grotesque, his face contorted in agony. But what other picture of God could have brought hope and salvation from self-pity and alienation to the inhabitants of Eisenheim, victims of a leprous skin disease which was the scourge of Europe in the late Middle Ages and took a terrible toll in disfigured bodies and broken spirits?

Then, too, the teachings of Jesus demand the Cross for a verification and certification. The ministry of one who taught forgiveness and reconciliation and love was in danger of floating away in a cloud of sentimentality and unreality. Some of the worst sins are the reactions of men to sins committed against them, and unless the chain reaction can be broken by some act of unmerited and unpredictable forgiveness, men must perish in a welter of bloody recriminations and revenge. So the critical and all-important test of a man's power to meet and overcome sin will be a situation in which, although wholly innocent, he is nevertheless shockingly and outrageously sinned against.

The illustrations in the Sermon on the Mount imagine such a situation. Here is what divine love means: to make no resistance to an unprovoked assault, to forgive those who without any justification are inflicting violence against one, to forgive the most outrageous offenses, not once and not seven times, but seventy times seven. Teaching like that made something like the cross on Calvary inevitable if the spoken words were ever to be believed. The Sermon on the Mount has often been dismissed as impossible and irrelevant. So it would be if it had not been tested once in bloody and brutal fact and its validity confirmed. Some forgiving act had to be interposed in the fatal chain reaction by which in actual human experience one sin begets another. A mere word or two about forgiveness, delivered in the atmosphere of a lecture on morality, never does anything to disinfect the blood stream of human existence from the accumulated hatreds and resentments of past sins.

The late Albert Camus saw that this was one of the appalling problems facing France as a result of the victory over Germany in 1944. In a speech in Paris in March, 1945, he described the problem with his usual eloquence.

We were left with hatred. We were left with the impulse that the other day in Dijon made a fourteen-year-old child fall upon a collaborator who had been lynched and disfigure his face. We were left with the rage that consumes our souls at the memory of certain images and certain faces. The executioner's hatred engendered the victim's hatred. And once the executioners had gone, the French were left with their hatred only partially spent. They still look at one another with a residue of anger. Well, this is what we must overcome first of all. Our poisoned hearts must be cured. And the most difficult battle to be won against the enemy in the future must be fought within ourselves, with an exceptional effort that will transform our appetite for hatred into a desire for justice.[2]

To a tortured and crushed people like the French in 1944, a few words about forgiveness spoken by even the most inspired teacher sound hollow and unconvincing and do nothing to penetrate to what Camus calls the poisoned heart. The teacher of the Mount of the Beatitudes secures a hearing only when he finds himself on the Mount of Cru-

cifixion, when nails pierce his own hands and thorns mar
his own brow, and sneering derision is the only response to
compassion and love; and precisely then and there he can
find the grace to speak of forgiveness, which otherwise
would have remained the epitome of ethereal irrelevance.

So by his baptism, his healings, and his teachings, the
Lord was from the outset of his career and ministry on the
way toward the Cross, and the significance of that central
event of his death and resurrection is given much of its
meaning and poignancy and power by the life which led
up to it.

Just how the Cross works to save man from his sin the
Church has never systematically—let alone, dogmatically
—defined. One of the Church's hymns says:

> I know not how that Calvary's cross
> A world from sin could free;
> I only know its matchless love
> Has brought God's love to me.

But although we shall never be able to give any definitive
theory of the Cross, we may be able to trace certain con-
nections between it and the sin of man and sin's forgiveness.

UNCONDITIONAL FORGIVENESS

The Cross is a demonstration, for example, of how com-
pletely forgiveness must take the initiative if it is to reach
and influence the sinful heart. The New Testament writers
are continually amazed at this capacity of the divine forgiveness to act not because of human repentance, but in

spite of human indifference. "While we were yet sinners Christ died for us." "Herein is love, not that we loved him but that he loved us and sent his son to be the propitiation for our sins." Nothing could more dramatically demonstrate the "in spite of" character of God's forgiveness than the Cross. Here forgiveness is offered in the midst of the very experience of rejection and vengeful persecution. The words recorded in St. Luke's Gospel emphasize how the divine mercy precedes and anticipates any slight suggestion of remorse or sorrow. "Father, forgive them for they know not what they do" was spoken on behalf of men who showed no hesitation whatsoever in carrying out their brutal work with hardhearted efficiency and complete indifference. How seldom men—even professedly Christian men—have grasped the miracle of this kind of forgiveness is illustrated by an address given by Generalissimo Francisco Franco at the end of the Spanish Civil War. Speaking to the defeated supporters of the Madrid government, he announced a policy of forgiveness. But, he was careful to say, this would not be what he called "liberal" forgiveness but Christian forgiveness, and the difference was that Christian forgiveness demanded first an abject acknowledgment by the sinner of his faults and a demonstrable determination to change his ways. When one reads this speech alongside Lincoln's Second Inaugural, it is not difficult to judge which one more fully understood the meaning of forgiveness in the New Testament. Christ crucified makes it clear how far God goes in initiating reconciliation between the sinner and the one sinned against. "When all was sin and shame, a second Adam to the fight and to the rescue came."

In his great sermon on the forgiven prostitute of St.
Luke's seventh chapter, Dr. Paul Tillich has given classical
expression to this amazing quality of divine forgiveness:

Forgiveness is unconditional or it is not forgiveness at all. Forgiveness has the character of "in spite of," but the righteous
ones give it the character of "because." The sinners, however,
cannot do this. . . . They cannot show facts because of
which they must be forgiven. . . . We know that this is our
situation, but we loathe to face it. It is too great as a gift and
too humiliating as a judgment. We want to contribute something, and if we have learned that we cannot contribute anything positive, then we try at least to contribute something
negative: the pain of self-accusation and self-rejection. . . .
God's forgiveness is independent of anything we do, even of
self-accusation and self-humiliation. If this were not so, how
could we ever be certain that our self-rejection is serious
enough to deserve forgiveness? Forgiveness creates repentance
—this is declared in our story and this is the experience of
those who have been forgiven.[3]

God does not offer men the forgiveness of the Cross after
they have come to him in contrition and remorse; he holds
out to them the forgiveness of the Cross as an initial gesture
in the hope that it may lead to a recognition of the depth
of their sin and make the path of repentance not a crushing
self-humiliation but a self-forgetful opening of the heart
to divine love.

THE CROSS AND THE COST OF SIN

It is clear also that forgiveness must be proclaimed by
one who suffers the penalties sin imposes, for otherwise
he would know nothing of the price forgiveness always

has to pay. The late Dag Hammarskjöld wrote in his remarkable diary under the date of Easter, 1960, the following words about forgiveness: "Forgiveness breaks the chain of causality because he who forgives you out of love takes upon himself the consequences of what you have done. Forgiveness, therefore, always entails a sacrifice." [4] It is easy to bandy about words about forgiveness, but such words may merely mean that the speaker has no realization whatever of the depths of suffering and the extent of destructiveness sin brings in its train. How can all the agony and loss be made up for? And unless it is made up for, somehow, is it not deeply immoral to wave a wand of forgiveness over the misdeeds and assure the perpetrator that everything is now quite all right? How did Jesus dare, for example, to forgive the notorious sinners he pardoned, apparently so freely and easily? They had left a trail of ruined ideals and blasted hopes and tarnished aspirations in their wake. How did he dare to tell the prostitute, for example, that her sins were forgiven? That was all right for him to say, but what about the cheapened and degraded understanding of sexual love that she had given currency to by her life, and what about the rising cost of self-control and marital fidelity for which her career was in part responsible? By what right can Jesus tell a grafting politician and tax collector that he can be of good cheer, for his sins are all wiped away, when their consequences in victimized unfortunates and in confirmed cynicism about the imperial justice still go on darkening the picture of human existence? Since sin inflicts suffering on the innocent, only one who was innocent and bore ultimate suffering—even to the point of being robbed of life itself—can dare to speak about removing its guilt.

JUDGED BY THE CROSS

So the forgiveness of the Cross has never been understood to be an invitation to sentimentality about sin. On the contrary, it has been a way of reminding men of what their sins cost and how catastrophic seemingly trivial shortcomings can turn out to be. "Sin's nature is made plain by that dying figure on the gibbet," Dr. Henry Sloane Coffin once wrote. "Sin is murderous to all we most admire. . . . Golgotha reminds us that ruinous forces reside in and dominate our world, that in men's spirits are suicidal tendencies which drive them to kill the God-like in themselves." [5]

At the same moment that the Cross offers forgiveness, it sharpens the outlines of sin in human life and lights up its appalling consequences. The consequences of some of the more obvious sins we have already noticed, but the sins which converged to create the catastrophe of Calvary were not the readily identified crimes against society of the prostitute and the thief and the rule breaker, but the respectable sins of the churchman, the patriot, the public official. Down through history the sins of caring for familiar orthodoxies, for traditional symbols of power and authority, for the façade of reputation and public esteem more than for justice and truth and human welfare have probably caused far more damage than the sins of flamboyance and sensuality.

In the late nineteenth century in France, a whole nation was torn between the partisans of the pride of the army and the stubborn defenders of a Jewish army captain,

Alfred Dreyfus. Even when evidence piled up that Dreyfus was innocent of the charges of espionage brought against him, the army resorted to forgery and suppression of evidence to bolster its case, on the grounds that a subverting of army discipline and a lowering of army prestige in the eyes of the people would result from admitting that an original mistake had been made. The historian D. W. Brogan describes one of the "Dreyfusards" who became convinced of the prisoner's innocence in these words:

Picquart was that rare type, a man who really cares for justice, no matter where his care for it may take him. He really did believe *fiat justitia ruat coelum* (let justice be done though the heavens fall), or it might be better to say he believed that righteousness exalteth a nation. . . . Justice for him involved a breach with the loyalties and beliefs of his whole life.[6]

The Cross is the prototype of all the crimes committed in the name of patriotism and national security and religious orthodoxy against the dignity and freedom and truth of human beings. That such crimes are still committed is clear when one hears, for example, that, apart from all other arguments about the policy of the United States in Vietnam, we must not change that policy since it would involve a loss of national prestige and of face. So Dr. Harold Bosley has written: "You not only killed him in A.D. 29 on Calvary outside the wall in Jerusalem—you have done it many times since. Every high hill in the world is a candidate for Calvary. And you know you would do it again if he were to come among you again." [7] The Cross obliges men to come face to face with the moral ambiguities of their own existence. Far from weakening or subverting the moral authority of the universe, it has done

more to trouble the human conscience and to make men
sensitive to the hidden "suicidal tendencies which drive
them to kill the God-like in themselves" than any other
event in human history. Where grace and mercy were
offered to men most persuasively and most boundlessly, sin
was also condemned most searchingly and most relent-
lessly. That is the paradox of the Cross—but also its great
power.

THE MEANING OF "SATISFACTION"

It is in this sense that Christian traditional theology has
spoken of a "satisfaction" for sin made at the Cross, a
phrase that has greatly troubled many modern thinkers.[8]
The classical formulation of this understanding of the
Cross was couched in terms which admittedly strike
harshly on modern ears, and yet one cannot escape the
impression that St. Anselm, its most thoroughgoing ex-
ponent, was talking about realities that we must take into
account in present experience. Anselm compared God to
a great feudal lord who had been slighted and affronted by
one of his serfs. The insult was not one that could be con-
doned, not even if the offender were subsequently repent-
ant and pleaded for forgiveness. In order that the honor
of the lord shall not be brought into disrepute—and with it
the whole structure of feudal authority—some "satisfaction" must be made.

It is not too difficult to translate this situation into
plausible contemporary terms. One can think, for example,
of the dilemma of an athletic team one of whose members
has been discovered, to the accompaniment of great pub-

licity, to have accepted a bribe to throw the game but who is thoroughly penitent and wishes to remain on the team and to redeem himself.[9] Why cannot the team extend its forgiveness and welcome his contrite return? The word "honor"—Anselm's word—is not too far from the mark to explain the problem the team would have with this line of action. "Honor" in this connection is not the hard-shelled and stiff pride which is unfeeling and unsympathetic to the erring member. It is a sense of the meaning of sportsmanship which demands a disowning of his betrayal of the standards of the game. One is reminded of a maxim of judicial practice—justice not only must be done but must be seen to be done. In the forgiveness of sins, God's honor is not really like the outraged pride of a feudal lord. It is more like the concern the team has that the standards of honest sportsmanship shall not be brought into disrepute and held in contempt.

If forgiveness were offered without "satisfaction," it would call into question the validity of the standards of life against which the sin was committed in the first place. If God were to say, in effect, "Forget it," then his principles of love and integrity would soon be forgotten too. To forgive by the sign and memory of the Cross is to ensure that the cost of sin is never forgotten or the price of mercy is never devalued. The strategy of the Cross, for example, would suggest that the athletic team accept the erring member back into its life but accompany this with an announcement that its star athlete would voluntarily withdraw from all games for a whole season. This is satisfaction, and it faces some of the deepest problems and puzzles which forgiveness raises.

THE MEANING OF THE CROSS IN OUR REDEMPTION

Much of what we have been saying is caught up in a sermon which was preached in the desperately dark days of Germany's approaching defeat by the great contemporary German pastor Helmut Thielicke.[10] To his congregation in Stuttgart on the morning after a devastating air raid which blew out the windows of the church and left it standing desolate amid the ruins of hundreds of homes and shops and schools under which were buried unnumbered dead relatives and friends, he chose to preach on this text from St. John: "And his disciples asked him, saying, 'Master, who did sin, this man or his parents, that he was born blind?' Jesus answered, 'Neither hath this man sinned, nor his parents: but that the works of God should be made manifest in him.'" (John 9:1-3) We must notice that Jesus, when he was confronted by the devastation and suffering which sin had wrought in human life, refused to speculate about relative responsibility for it but asked instead what could be achieved out of it. The man's blindness may have been due to his own fault or to his parents' fault—in line with the theology of the time. In some contexts this is an important question, but unless it is to become a source of obsessive guilt or desperate defiance, it must be superseded finally by the deeper question: To what purpose can all this suffering and desolation be turned? Here was what Pastor Thielicke told his Stuttgart congregation, some of whom had perhaps already heard terrible rumors of the crimes of their national leadership. His words do nothing to deny their guilt, but they point beyond that to a deeper truth about life and about God.

Perhaps you are given the task to live for others more than you ever did when life was secure. Could you really have understood their needs if you yourself had not been plunged into these depths? Wounds must heal wounds. True helpers of their fellow men have always been those who were greatly hurt, who had to suffer great sorrows. Jesus could be our Pastor, our great High Priest—only because He Himself had to stand against the forces of guilt and suffering and death and thus He could have sympathy with those who sit in the shadow of those powers.[11]

The Cross makes it possible to face the deepest and darkest consequences of sin's power and to think with gratitude of the works of God that may be made manifest even in this desperate experience.

Professor John H. Randall, of Columbia University, has pointed out that, according to Aristotle's classic definition, "Calvary would not be a tragedy." [12] Aristotle warned the ambitious tragedian that he must not depict the protagonist of his play as a thoroughly good man who is then "shown passing from prosperity to misfortune." [13] The reason is that the average onlooker would be offended by the brutality of such a situation and would not then experience the "pity and terror"—the reaction which, for Aristotle, defines a true tragedy. Greek tragedy dealt with heroes whose suffering resulted usually from some "tragic flaw" in their characters. Clearly, this is not true of the story of Jesus and his Cross. But then, perhaps the aim of the story is very different from the aim Aristotle assumed for tragedy. Our reaction to Calvary is not meant to be one of "pity and terror." The liturgical observances of Good Friday must not be allowed to become an occasion for an annual good cry, for example, though one will not be unmoved at the spectacle of divine love rebuffed and thrust out of the way. There may not be enough terror, as a matter of fact, in our contemporary Good Friday observances. The ancient ceremony of Tenebrae, with the congregation watching as the lights of the candles are extinguished one by one and the church plunged into darkness, has much to recommend it as suggesting the terror which, according to the Gospels, nature itself manifested at the sight of the Cross. But "terror" cannot be the chief purpose of Good Friday either.

The New Testament sees the Cross as the first stage in the great process of man's death and resurrection. He who hung on it two thousand years ago died not only the death of the body but died also and more importantly to the usual preoccupations with self-importance and self-justification. "In that he died, he died unto sin once." We are not to watch the spectacle simply in terror and pity but to believe that the only way to be saved from sin is to share his death to self. When heartbreaking, disappointing, and agonizing suffering beset us, God is asking us whether we are ready to trust him as the Crucified One trusted him and to let our existence find its genuine meaning in his providence and overruling power. In a rather deeper sense than it is usually meant, we may say, "In the midst of life we are in death." St. Paul understood that his life was a daily dying to sin, to anxious self-concern and ruthless self-promotion. The Man on the Cross represents the startling truth about human existence: that it realizes its greatest glory when it allows God to make whatever use he thinks best of all its achievements and undertakings. From the anxious Adam who snatched at life's possibilities in defiance and ruthlessness, we are asked to turn our hearts and minds toward another model of what it means to be a man: to the second Adam, who trusts life and the God within it and meets its responsibilities with a knowledge of his fallibility and finitude but with the assurance that nothing done in this spirit is ever done in vain.

CHAPTER EIGHT

New Life Beyond Forgiveness

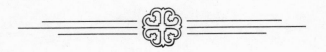

IT HAS often been said that if Calvary were the end of the story of Jesus Christ, there never would have been any Christian Church or any Christian religion. To be somewhat more specific, if there had been no Easter, there would have been no assurance of God's forgiveness of sins nor of his power to create new life out of the ruins of sin's devastation. Easter is as much about sin as it is about death, as much about the new life beyond forgiveness as it is about the new life beyond the tomb. St. Paul always links the proclamation of the Resurrection with a confident promise about God's triumphant dealings with sin. ". . . Jesus our Lord, who was delivered up because of the sins we had committed, and raised up because of the justification that was to be granted us." (Rom. 4:24*b*-25)[1] Elsewhere St. Paul is even more explicit: "If Christ is not risen, all your faith is a delusion; you are back in your sins." (1 Cor. 15:17 NEB)

A recent playwright, Dorothy Sayers, has caught the

atmosphere of an Easterless Christianity in one of her radio
plays, the setting of which is the Zebedees' house in Jerusalem an hour before dawn on the "first day of the week."
There is a soft knocking on the door as the scene opens:

JOHN: Is that you, Mary?

MARY MAGDALEN: Yes, John.

JOHN: Come in . . . How did you find them all at Bethany?

MARY MAGDALEN: With heart and spirit broken. But a little
    comforted to know that all of us were safe . . . Peter is
    here with you?

JOHN: Like a sick animal that has crawled home to die. He
    can't eat. He can't sleep. He can't forgive himself. It was my
    fault. I knew he was frightened, yet I left him alone in the
    house of Annas. Dear Lord! was there none of us you could
    trust for five minutes?

MARY MAGDALEN: Poor Peter. He takes his failures hard.

JOHN: He calls himself a worse traitor than . . . I can't speak
    the name. I can't say our Master's prayer. "Forgive us our
    trespasses as we forgive"—no it's impossible . . . You heard
    what became of him?

MARY MAGDALEN: Yes. John, you can't hate him worse than
    he came to hate himself. His self-hate murdered him.

JOHN (*slowly*): If I hate him, I am his murderer too . . . O
    God! there is no end to our sins! Do we all murder Jesus
    and one another? [2]

THE DIFFERENCE THE RESURRECTION MAKES

Here is what Christianity would have been—if it had
survived at all—without the Resurrection: a melancholy,
guilt-ridden, self-accusing recollection of a man who spoke
about mercy and forgiveness and love but who was destroyed by vengeance and suspicion and fear, and whose

death, therefore, leaves men more remorseful and bitter against themselves and against one another than ever before. "If Christ is not risen, all your faith is a delusion; you are back in your sins."

A familiar accusation against the Christian doctrine of the resurrection of the dead is that it is a presumptuous piece of self-conceit. That appears to be unanswerable unless the resurrection of Christ first of all does something about the problem of our sin. It would be an appalling prospect: an eternity of millions of human creatures, all anxiously and nervously promoting themselves and insisting on their own importance. It would be difficult to imagine a situation more desperate than an endless lifetime of making excuses, trying to justify one's mistakes, bolstering one's reputation, proving over and over again one's superiority and virtue. Such an existence could only be described as hell—which is exactly what the classical theologies called it.

George Bernard Shaw once thought he had refuted the Christian doctrine of resurrection from the dead by the observation that he found the idea of an eternity of himself an intolerable one. Any man, of course, with any objectivity and sense of humor might say the same thing about himself, especially if he possessed Shaw's gift of devastating brilliance. Shaw, however, missed the point. The Resurrection was, first of all, the resurrection of Jesus Christ. It was not an assurance that the fearful, squabbling, anxious apostles would go on like that forever. The Resurrection has to be able to make a difference in man's inner life, has to cut the nerve of his anxiety and self-concern, has to free him from self-preoccupation and guilt so that he is able to serve and love others—and then its promise that such an emancipated and fulfilled life triumphs over death is great good news. C. S. Lewis, in his famous book *The Great Divorce*, imagines a bus which makes a daily trip from hell to heaven, and any of the denizens of hell may come along if they want and stay if they want. The fact turns out to be that most of them, having chosen self-centeredness, find a realm of self-forgetfulness intolerable and unbearable and head back to hell with a sigh of relief. It is not good news to announce that God has provided a free bus trip to heaven. The Resurrection must have some power to transform man's arrogant, anxious, fearful self-centeredness into the trusting, loving compassion of Christ. Indeed, St. John says, when that kind of a transformation can be seen to have begun, we have already passed from death unto life.

This transformation begins when the love of God, amazingly manifested at the Cross, is seen to have ultimate power and authority in the Resurrection. The Resurrection rescues the Cross from being a futile and pathetic gesture, for the Resurrection shows us what God can make out of the disaster of sin and why, therefore, he can dare to forgive it. We have already noticed the audacity of Jesus' claim to forgive sins. It astounded his contemporaries and, if we really felt the tragedy of sin as our forefathers did, it would astound us too. His license to do it was finally given in the Resurrection. Again and again in the earliest Christian sermons, samples of which are given us in the Acts of the Apostles, the fact of Christ's resurrection is closely associated with his power to forgive sin. Part of the reason for this connection was that the Resurrection identified Jesus as the Divine Lord, the one who bears the authority of God himself, who, as we tried to show in Chapter 6, is alone authorized to speak forgiveness on behalf of the whole structure of reality. So St. Peter says to the Pentecost crowd, "God has made this Jesus, whom ye crucified, both Lord and Messiah. . . . Repent and be baptized, every one of you, in the name of Jesus the Messiah for the forgiveness of sins." (Acts 2:36-38 NEB) Another sermon, however, carries the argument a step further, for it says in effect, "You committed a deep and terrible crime in the crucifixion; the Resurrection shows you how terrible it was, for it identifies your victim as God's own Messiah. But what you did in criminal ignorance has been taken in hand by God, and by it He has 'fulfilled what he had foretold in the utterances of all the prophets: that his Messiah should suffer. Repent then and turn to God, so that your sins may be wiped out.' " (Acts 3:18-19 NEB)

SIN NOT AN IRRETRIEVABLE DISASTER

The importance of the first Easter for the Christian practice and proclamation of sin's forgiveness is that it has shown that sin is not irretrievably a disaster, but that God can make something of it which is constructive and redeeming. If Jesus the Messiah had really been destroyed by the sin of men, then all he ever said about forgiveness would have been lost in the recriminations and accusations of apostles and high priests and Roman authorities—not the least of which would have been the self-accusations of the apostles themselves. John would have gone on hating Judas, and Peter could never have made an end of hating himself. In the Easter light it was clear that God used the sins of all of them—whether the sins of weakness and ignorance or the sins of desperation and pride—to work the great blessing of Jesus' glorification as Saviour and Lord. For all the reasons we have considered in Chapter 7, "was the Messiah not bound to suffer thus before entering upon his glory?" (Luke 24:26) Only if the sinner begins to see that the divine resourcefulness can create something out of his sin can he ever be persuaded that he can be forgiven. In her play *The Zeal of Thy House,* Dorothy Sayers imagines a stonemason working on an intricate carving for the choir of Canterbury Cathedral who clumsily lets his tool slip and spoils the whole great piece of stone. The architect, however, takes the tool out of his hand and, although he rebukes him for his clumsiness, begins also to enact forgiveness. He fashions out of the spoiled carving a new, grotesque gargoyle which has its own part to play in the ensemble of the Cathedral. "So works with us," concludes Dorothy Sayers, "the cunning craftsman, God."

This is the reason why St. Augustine had the boldness to cry, "O felix culpa"—*O happy sin!* It is not the sort of cry one might expect from a genuinely penitent saint, and yet the Resurrection makes it altogether appropriate. The new life beyond forgiveness can find reason for rejoicing even in one's sins! As Dr. Austin Farrer has pointed out, this can be true without for a moment suggesting that the sin is "a positive gain to our Creator." He suggests two possible meanings of Augustine's "O felix culpa!" One could be stated like this: "It would have been an absolute disaster if [St. Augustine] had been able from the beginning to embrace the religion in which St. Monica reared him. Augustine the innocent could never, on this view, have been so perfect a soul as Augustine the penitent actually proved to be." ³

Farrer is troubled by this way of putting it, for it seems to make sin a *necessary* part of a man's pathway to God. It is not *necessary* to sin in order that grace may abound. True, St. Augustine's turbulent life, his violent plunges into sensuality, his arrogant attempts to establish the validity of his own reasoning, all of this made him the man he was later as a Christian. His thought would not have carried poignancy and conviction nor expressed the depths of man's sinfulness and the wonder of God's power and grace if his early career had not been what it was. But there are other kinds of sainthood besides the Augustinian sort, and he might have been an even greater Christian—though quite different—if his earlier life had been spared some of its torments and vicissitudes. What we can say in explanation of "felix culpa" is phrased by Farrer like this: "In retrospect [Augustine] found the leading of God's hand in all the wandering of his steps, for these roundabout paths had brought him to a saving faith. . . . Let us say that God would never have allowed evils to subsist in his creation, were it not that he might find in them the occasion to produce good things unique in kind and dependent for their unique character upon the evils in question." ⁴

So, like St. Paul, we can "give thanks in all things"—even in the knowledge of our sin. Because Easter proved that human sin—far from destroying Jesus—was employed by God to release the power of his life into the hearts of all men everywhere, John can forgive Judas, and Peter can forgive himself, and we can all, despite our unworthiness and folly, be bold enough to claim fellowship with him as Master and Lord.

THE MEANING OF NEW LIFE

The prayer of General Confession uses three words to describe the new life beyond forgiveness: "That we may hereafter live a godly, righteous, and sober life." (See Titus 2:11-12: "For the grace of God that bringeth salvation hath appeared to all men, teaching us that denying ungodliness and worldly lusts, we should live soberly, righteously and godly in this present world.") The new life is a life which more than ever before finds its meaning, its defense, its justification, its power, in a relationship with God. When a man has died to self, that is to say, when he has faced the fact that nothing he does is quite honest enough, quite pure enough, quite sacrificial enough, quite wise or virtuous enough, to meet the demands life puts upon him, he is ready to find the meaning of his life in God and to discover that God alone can be trusted for results man could never foresee, for responses man could never earn, for triumphs man could never win by his own wit or power. To have been forgiven at the Cross and born again in the power of Christ's resurrection is to know that we owe our lives far more to God than to ourselves. The new life beyond forgiveness is a godly life.

One of the important consequences of such godliness is a surprising freedom from both the threats and the promises by which the world seeks to coerce and control and direct us. The man who must prove his own virtue and establish his own security anxiously seeks the world's approval and covets the world's rewards. Only by the buttressing of the ego which such endorsement provides is modern man sustained in his quest for significance and value. A sign of this anxiety is the prevalence of the word "image" in modern public relations. The impression conveyed counts for everything. Contrast the freedom of a man like St. Paul from such preoccupations. "If I am called to account by you or by any human court of judgment, it does not matter to me in the least. Why, I do not even pass judgment on myself, for I have nothing on my conscience; but that does not mean I stand acquitted. My judge is the Lord." (1. Cor. 4:4 NEB) God searches more deeply than the world, demands an inner integrity—as we have already noticed— which the world seldom requires; but God also judges more understandingly, more mercifully, and so his judgments can be trusted and relied upon to deal with the realities of the self in a way that the world's judgments do not customarily manage to do.

In an earlier period of the Church's life, this godliness found dramatic exemplification in the lives of the great ascetics. It is not a style of Christian life now much in vogue—unless one accepts as parallels the carelessness about dress and personal appearance practiced among some of the younger intellectuals and artists. St. Anthony of Egypt might well pass unnoticed in Greenwich Village in New York or North Beach in San Francisco. We may regard such carelessness with distaste, but at least among the ascetics of the past, it often represented an achievement of godliness that resulted in breath-taking freedom from

the things which usually control and determine our behavior. One story is told of the appearance before the
emperor's magistrate of the great St. Basil, arraigned on a
charge of having resisted the emperor's regulations about
the correct form of Christian belief. Since Basil seemed
self-possessed and quite unintimidated, the magistrate reminded him:

"I can confiscate your possessions, banish you, torture you,
put you to death." "Is that all?" answered the saint. "None of
these things trouble me. You cannot confiscate my possessions,
for I have none, unless you want to take the threadbare clothes
I am wearing, and the few books in my library. Banishment—
exile—what have these to do with me? Everywhere on God's
earth I am at home! You cannot exile me from the grace of
God, and wherever I am cast forth, there I am a stranger and a
pilgrim. Torture cannot touch me, for I no longer have a body
to torture; and is there any torture in being put to death with
a single blow, for that is the only power you have over me.
As for death, it is welcome to me, for it will bring me sooner
into His blessed Presence, close to Him whom I serve. Further-
more I am for the most part already dead and have long been
hurrying to the grave." 5

Before we deride the asceticism of the monastic life as
St. Basil practiced it, consider the freedom it gave him to
be a godly man. In such men, St. Paul's words are fulfilled,
"Ye are dead, and your life is hid with Christ in God."
(Col. 3:3)

RIGHTEOUSNESS IN A NEW KEY

The new life beyond forgiveness is a life of righteousness
—righteousness in a new key, righteousness with a saving

difference. Jesus must have shaken his hearers when he said, "Except your righteousness shall exceed the righteousness of the scribes and Pharisees, ye shall in no case enter into the kingdom of heaven." What can it mean to exceed the righteousness of the men who above anyone else in first-century Judaism or since were serious and scrupulous about moral values? The strain of later controversy led some of the New Testament writers to do less than justice to the Pharisees. A parable of Jesus' gives us a truer insight into what they were at their best. The Pharisee, praying in the temple, gives what is intended to be a fair picture of his own moral status: "I am not . . . an extortioner, unjust, an adulterer. . . . I fast twice in the week, I give tithes of all that I possess." It might be well to pause to reflect on what an impressive record this is. The man is honest in his business dealings, sets fair prices, gives value for value received. He is a model husband, faithful and loyal to his marriage vows. To top it all, he is an exemplary churchman, devout in his religious duties and astonishingly generous in supporting the church budget. He would seem to be the answer to a pastor's prayer! How, one asks in bewilderment, can anyone's righteousness "exceed" that? The answer lies in a few deceptively innocent words which we have omitted in our paraphrase of the Pharisee's prayer. What he really said was, "God, I thank thee, that I am not *as other men are* . . . even as this publican."

Righteousness is spoiled by the very efforts men make to sustain and improve it. We saw in Chapter 4 how subtly our very best efforts are tainted and twisted and corrupted. The Pharisee's righteousness separated and isolated him from other people, prompted him to make invidious com-

parisons, led him to disparage others, to be insensitive to
their temptations and perplexities. If the meaning of righteousness is love, a love which unites men and identifies
them with one another, then here is a paradox: righteousness is self-defeating. But the forgiven sinner has found
a way out of that paradox. The things that usually spoil
human righteousness—condescension, complacency, dom-
ineering interference in the other's liberty—all the alienat-
ing things we call "self-righteousness" have had their root
cut by the humiliation of having to go on God's charity
list and to accept our status as a gift from the one whom
we put to death again and again by our sins. Because the
forgiven sinner is godly—that is to say, finds his life and
its justification in God—he has discovered the secret of a
righteousness that exceeds any self-congratulatory morality.

The forgiven sinner is said to lead a life which is sober.
Sober is not a very exciting word; it suggests life in a low
key. The ancient Greeks advised a virtue that might be
called sobriety—*sophrosune*, the knowledge that one's for-
tunes may change and so one ought not to count on life
too much. Herodotus tells us that the wisdom of Solon
which he tried to teach Croesus was that no man can be
counted happy until after his life is over, since life may
at any time bring human happiness crashing down in ruin
and disaster. To lead a sober life meant to the Greeks to
practice a certain kind of detachment, not to care too
much about anything, not to expect too much of existence.
This can scarcely be what the New Testament means by
a sober life. As a matter of fact, when we meet the Christians of the New Testament, we notice an intensity and

an ardor and an eagerness of expectation which Herodotus would have deplored as excessive and irrational. To live a sober life means for a Christian to live a life of great expectation—but an expectation based on the promise and the faithfulness and the love of God. A Christian man knows too much about his own sins to expect too much of his own plans and ambitions. Too often he has seen his good intentions miscarry and his most hopeful projects betrayed by some failure of his own sensitivity or integrity. He has spoiled life too often to face it with unbounded optimism. But he has been forgiven so much and has found life offering so many of its joys and opportunities to him again and again, despite his many failures, that he possesses a boldness about life that Herodotus would have found puzzling and inexplicable.

THE REALITY OF CHRISTIAN HOPE

Two modern plays, widely different in style and philosophical background, nevertheless have a similar understanding of the sober life. They are T. S. Eliot's *The Cocktail Party* and Edward Albee's *Who's Afraid of Virginia Woolf?* [6] In both plays the focus of attention is an unhappily married couple: Edward and Lavinia are more conventional in their unhappiness; George and Martha turn the air blue with their language. Both couples, however, find a new kind of communion and understanding through a process which might well be called "death and rebirth." For Edward and Lavinia it takes the form of the failure for both of them of love affairs with others. For George and Martha it is the explosion of the private fiction of a child of their marriage. In both cases, the collapse of the façade of the marriage promises to be the beginning of a new and more sober and genuine relationship. Mr. Eliot is explicit in his analysis in a scene with the somewhat mysterious psychiatrist, Sir Henry Harcourt-Reilly:

EDWARD: Lavinia, we must make the best of a bad job. That is what he means.
REILLY: When you find, Mr. Chamberlayne,
The best of a bad job is all any of us makes of it . . .
              . . . You will forget this phrase
And in forgetting it will alter the condition.[7]

Mr. Albee is more subtle. As the guest, Nick, senses the truth of the situation and asks, "You couldn't have . . . any?", George says, "*We* couldn't," and Martha, with Mr. Albee's stage direction (*A hint of communion*), is made to echo his words, "*We* couldn't." When Nick and Honey leave, the "hint of communion" is more firmly established:

GEORGE: It will be better.
MARTHA: I don't . . . know.
GEORGE: It will be . . . maybe.
MARTHA: I'm . . . not . . . sure.
GEORGE: No.
MARTHA: Just . . . us?
GEORGE: Yes.
MARTHA: I don't suppose, maybe, we could . . .
GEORGE: No, Martha.[8]

The failures of married love cannot be miraculously overcome, but the understanding of the reality of forgiveness—in Mr. Eliot, specific in its Christian origin and implications; in Mr. Albee, naturalized and secularized—enables life to go on in even deeper and more authentic ways. This is the meaning of the blessing which the risen Christ gave to the disciples. They were broken, as Dorothy Sayers's play suggests, by the depth of their failure and inadequacy; but he says to them with authority and assurance, "Peace be unto you." St. John anticipates this post-Easter blessing in the discussions at the Last Supper, in which Jesus makes clear that this peace of his is given not as the world gives peace. It is a peace which comes to a man on the far side of the most dreadful and sickening failures and the most costly blunders. One would not dare claim it for himself. The Victim of Calvary, the Victor of Easter, alone can bestow it and be believed and trusted. Human existence is strewn with the wreckage of sin. Despite it—on the basis of it—new life can arise, begotten by the divine mercy, nourished by human penitence, crowned and fulfilled by the gifts which man can trust God finally to bestow. This is the Christian faith and the Christian hope by which Christian charity gains its strength and resiliency and power. This is the secret of the art of being a sinner.

Notes

FOR CHAPTER 1: Sin in the Sixties

[1] Harvey Cox, *The Secular City* (New York: Macmillan, 1965), pp. 80-81. [2] Joseph Fletcher, *Situational Ethics, the New Morality* (Philadelphia: Westminster, 1966), p. 81. [3] Alexander Miller, *The Renewal of Man* (New York: Doubleday, 1955), pp. 99-100. [4] Joseph Fletcher, *op. cit.*, p. 124. [5] T. S. Eliot, *The Cocktail Party* (New York: Harcourt, 1950), p. 132.

FOR CHAPTER 2: The God to Whom We Confess

[1] Albert Camus, *The Fall*, trans. by Justin O'Brien (New York: Knopf, 1957), p. 47. [2] D. R. Davies, *Down Peacock's Feathers* (London and New York: Macmillan, 1944). [3] H. H. Munro, *The Short Stories of Saki* (New York: Viking, 1941), pp. 691-693.

FOR CHAPTER 3: The Grandeur and Misery of Sin

[1] C. S. Lewis, *The Screwtape Letters* (New York: Macmillan, 1943). [2] Robert Penn Warren, *Brother to Dragons* (New

York: Random House, 1953), p. 111. [3] *The Collected Poetry of W. H. Auden* (New York: Random House, 1945), p. 165. [4] Herbert Butterfield, *Christianity, Diplomacy, and War* (Nashville: Abingdon, 1953).

FOR CHAPTER 4: How Sinful Are We?

[1] Stephen Bayne, *In the Eyes of the Lord* (New York: Harpers, 1958), p. 143. [2] Søren Kierkegaard, *Philosophical Fragments or a Fragment of Philosophy*, trans. by David F. Swenson (Princeton, N.J.: Princeton University Press, 1936), p. xiii. [3] H. A. Williams, *The True Wilderness* (London: Constable, 1965), p. 89. [4] *Ibid.*, p. 90.

FOR CHAPTER 5: The Hopefulness of Being Sorry

[1] T. S. Eliot, *op. cit.*, p. 132. [2] Alexander Miller, *op. cit.*, p. 72. [3] Dorothy L. Sayers, *The Man Born to Be King* (London: Gollancz, 1946), p. 335. [4] Hughell E. W. Fosbroke, *By Means of Death* (New York: Seabury, 1956), p. 29. [5] Christopher Fry, *The Dark Is Light Enough* (New York: Oxford, 1954), p. 20.

FOR CHAPTER 6: Who Shall Deliver Me?

[1] William Hamilton, "The Death of God Theologies Today," in Thomas Altizer and William Hamilton, *Radical Theology and the Death of God* (New York: Bobbs-Merrill, 1966), p. 41. [2] See, for example, James A. Pike, *What Is This Treasure?* (New York: Harpers, 1966), Chaps. 6-7. It is true that Bishop Pike refers to the experience of the Christian community with Jesus, but he does not say explicitly what so much of the New Testament confesses: "Him hath God exalted with his right hand to be a Prince and a Saviour, for to give repentance to Israel, and forgiveness of sin" (Acts 5:31). [3] See the illuminating and clarifying essay by R. A. Norris, Jr., "Toward a Contemporary Interpretation of the Chalcedonian *Definition*," in

Lux in Lumine: Essays to Honor W. Norman Pittenger, ed. by R. A. Norris, Jr. (New York: Seabury, 1966). [4] H. E. Bettenson, *Documents of the Christian Church* (2nd ed.; New York: Oxford, 1963), p. 64. [5] William Hamilton, *op. cit.,* p. 35. [6] Hugh Montefiore, *A Commentary on the Epistle to the Hebrews* (New York: Harpers, 1964), p. 91. [7] Thornton Wilder, *The Angel That Troubled the Waters* (New York: Coward-McCann, 1928), pp. 147-149. [8] Gustav Aulén, *Christus Victor,* trans. by A. G. Hebert (New York: Macmillan, 1954). [9] I owe this illuminating illustration to a lecture delivered by another Swedish theologian, Anders Nygren, at the Yale Divinity School in the spring of 1948. [10] H. A. Williams, *op. cit.,* pp. 102-103.

FOR CHAPTER 7: Rescued by a Cross

[1] Albert Camus, in *The Fall,* imagines Jesus being haunted by the slaughter of the innocents. His own life had cost the lives of thousands of children. How can a man live with a burden like that, Camus asks. [2] Albert Camus, *Resistance, Rebellion, and Death,* trans. by Justin O'Brien (New York: Knopf, 1961), pp. 62-63. [3] Paul Tillich, "To Whom Much Is Forgiven . . . ," in *The New Being* (New York: Scribners, 1955), pp. 8-9. [4] Dag Hammarskjöld, *Markings* (New York: Knopf, 1964), p. 197. [5] Henry Sloane Coffin, *The Meaning of the Cross* (New York: Scribners, 1959), pp. 89-90. [6] D. W. Brogan, *The Development of Modern France, 1870-1939,* rev. ed. (New York: Harper Torchbooks, 1966, Vol. I), p. 330. [7] Harold Bosley, quoted in *The Christian Century* (March 30, 1966), p. 387. [8] See, e.g., James A. Pike, *op. cit.,* p. 81, where the Prayer Book phrase which speaks of Christ on the Cross having made "a full, perfect, and sufficient sacrifice, oblation, and satisfaction for the sins of the whole world" is criticized because it "implicitly attributes to God a morality we deplore in his creatures: the requirement of a 'pay-off,' a 'pound of flesh.' " [9] This illustration is suggested by a few lines in Leon-

ard Hodgson's *The Doctrine of the Atonement* (New York:
Scribners, 1951), p. 58. For another illustration, see my
Modern Heresies (New York: Seabury, 1961), pp. 134-136.
¹⁰ Helmut Thielicke, "The God of Ends," in *Out of the
Depths,* trans. by G. W. Bromiley (Grand Rapids, Mich.:
Eerdmans, 1962), pp. 9-20. ¹¹ *Ibid.,* p. 18. ¹² John H. Randall,
Aristotle (New York: Columbia University Press, 1960), p.
293. ¹³ *Aristotle, Containing Selections from Seven of the Most
Important Books, etc.,* trans. by Philip Wheelwright (New
York: Odyssey, 1935), p. 306.

FOR CHAPTER 8: New Life Beyond Forgiveness

¹ As trans. by C. K. Barrett in *A Commentary on the Epistle to
the Romans* (New York: Harpers, 1957), p. 93. ² Dorothy L.
Sayers, *op. cit.,* pp. 323-324. ³ Austin Farrer, *Love Almighty
and Ills Unlimited* (New York: Doubleday, 1961), p. 143.
⁴ *Ibid.,* pp. 142, 144. ⁵ Robert Payne, *The Holy Fire* (New
York: Harpers, 1957), p. 129. ⁶ This parallel was noted in a
discussion between Dean Robert Corrigan, of New York University, and the Reverend Nicholas Holt, of Holyrood Church,
New York City, in a program at the Church of the Ascension
during Lent, 1966. ⁷ T. S. Eliot, *op. cit.,* p. 126. ⁸ Edward
Albee, *Who's Afraid of Virginia Woolf?* (New York: Atheneum, 1962), pp. 138, 140-141.